NAPOLI
on the road

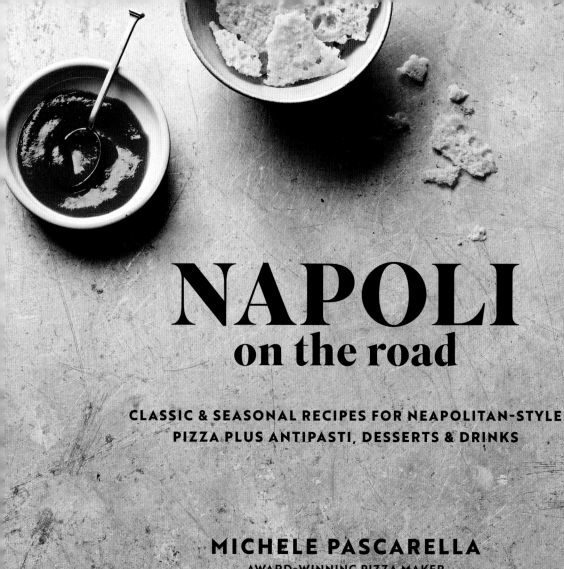

NAPOLI
on the road

CLASSIC & SEASONAL RECIPES FOR NEAPOLITAN-STYLE
PIZZA PLUS ANTIPASTI, DESSERTS & DRINKS

MICHELE PASCARELLA
AWARD-WINNING PIZZA MAKER

PHOTOGRAPHY BY STEVEN JOYCE

RYLAND PETERS & SMALL
LONDON • NEW YORK

Senior Designer Megan Smith
Senior Editor Gillian Haslam
Head of Production
  Patricia Harrington
Editorial Director Julia Charles
Creative Director
  Leslie Harrington

Pizza maker Michele Pascarella
Food stylist Jess Geddes
Drinks stylist Andrea Principessa
Prop stylist Hannah Wilkinson
Contributing writer
  Rosario Dello Iacovo
Indexer Hilary Bird

First published in 2025 by
Ryland Peters & Small
20–21 Jockey's Fields
London WC1R 4BW
and
1452 Davis Bugg Road
Warrenton, NC 27589
www.rylandpeters.com

10 9 8 7 6 5 4 3 2 1

Text copyright © Michele
Pascarella 2025

Design and photography
copyright © Ryland Peters & Small
2025

See page 176 for full credits

ISBN: 978-1-78879-644-6

A CIP record for this book is
available from the British Library.

US Library of Congress
cataloguing-in-publication data
has been applied for.

Printed and bound in China

NOTES

· Both American (Imperial plus
US cups) and British (Metric)
measurements and ingredients
are included in these recipes for
your convenience, however it is
important to work with one set of
measurements and not alternate
between the two within a recipe.

· All spoon measurements are
level unless otherwise specified.

· The author recommends that
liquid ingredients for pizza dough
are weighed in g/oz rather than
measured by volume. The use
of digital scales for this purpose
is highly recommended.

· Uncooked or partially cooked
eggs should not be served to
the very old, frail, young children,
pregnant women or those with
compromised immune systems.

· A note about cheese: Most
authentic varieties of Pecorino
and Parmesan use animal
rennet in their PDO-protected
production processes (usually
sheep rennet). This means
that they aren't suitable for
vegetarians. Pecorino- and
Parmesan-style cheeses made
with vegetarian rennet are
available, so check the label and
buy what works for you. Fior di
latte and mozzarella are generally
made with a non-animal rennet,
but again it's a good idea to check
the label carefully if in any doubt.

contents

introduction

As I lift the World's Best Pizza Chef 2023 trophy from 50 Top Pizza, having been crowned the world's best pizza maker, it is my hands that remind me I am not dreaming. It all started with the sense of touch, as my fingers first dipped into flour, testing its soft texture. I soon discovered that adding a bit of water created a dough that could be rolled out and shaped. This was my first pizza experiment, and I was just 11 years old. It was then that I knew I wanted to dedicate my life to making pizza and nothing else.

My brother-in-law was a pizza maker, and I began spending my spare time in the pizzeria where he worked, a place called Grano Cotto in Maddaloni, Caserta, which no longer exists. By watching, asking questions and trying it myself, I eventually started working there. I was learning to make pizzas and my old boss, to help me understand the value and the importance of food, told me 'you have one chance to make your pizza, if you burn the pizza or destroy it, you will not eat any pizza tonight'. This taught me that food is precious and should not be wasted.

I didn't only practise making pizza but also worked in the main kitchen. This background allows me to create recipes and understand the flavours I put on my pizzas. Many pizza makers today lack these skills, preventing them from fully appreciating how to balance ingredients, timing, cooking, colours, flavours, acidity and bitterness – essential elements for making a proper pizza.

This first phase of my life in Italy ended in June 2011. I left school and headed for Cornwall in the UK to see something of the world beyond my small hometown. After three months in Truro, I returned to Italy briefly before eventually heading to London. London was a turning point. The city offered me opportunities I am forever grateful for. My Neapolitan pizza, born in London and incorporating British ingredients, owes much to this great city. This unique blend enabled me to win a world competition, even surpassing pizza makers in Naples, the pizza capital of the world.

When I arrived in London, I had no money but found work at Sartori, a historic Italian restaurant. I stayed there for four and a half years, teaching myself about dough, different types of flour and the importance of water, salt and leavening. I discovered that a long leavening time of up to 36 hours produces a lighter pizza with a naturally pronounced crust. The customers were happy, and so were the owners, as many people ordered two or even three pizzas.

I had achieved a goal, but I always wondered what the next step would be. At Sartori, I became an integral part of the process, but I wanted to be in charge of the process. That's when the idea for Napoli On The Road was born. Along with another pizza maker from Sartori, we embarked on a new adventure. We counted our money, analyzed the market and realized that with our limited resources, we could only open a street-food business. My investment was relatively small, lent to me by my girlfriend, who in turn took out a bank loan.

We went to Sicily and bought a Piaggio Ape, a small three-wheeled van reminiscent of the one Gregory Peck drove in the movie *Roman Holiday*. We had a wood-burning oven mounted on it, and in January 2016, Napoli On The Road was born.

The beginning was tough. On our first day, we sold 27 pizzas, and I was thrilled. But we soon realized this wasn't enough to cover our expenses. We had to grow and persevere. I made the dough by hand at home, woke up at 5 am, loaded the van and drove around selling pizzas. In the evening, I worked shifts in other pizzerias. It was a gruelling life that lasted six months, but then came another turning point.

I suggested trying farmers' markets to my business partner. He was sceptical at first, but I was convinced it was the next step. Our first market in Wembley, close to the football stadium, saw us selling 90 pizzas, a new record. Our numbers kept rising until the market managers asked us to cover their other three markets. We accepted, and at Imperial College, we sold 150 pizzas on our first day — a new milestone.

The real breakthrough came at the One New Change shopping centre in London's St Paul's. After a month and a half, we were averaging 300 pizzas a day, becoming the market's culinary stars. Our success was so significant that large companies paying millions in rent found their restaurants empty, while we paid just a meagre amount in rent each week. They eventually pushed us out. A vacant space in the shopping centre became available and I wanted to take it, but my partner thought it too risky and ultimately we went our separate ways.

In 2018, I continued on my own, feeling it was time for another step. By September 2019, Napoli On The Road transformed into a restaurant. I opened in Chiswick, west London, and the decision to invest in a culturally vibrant, cosmopolitan area paid off. Customers recognized that my pizza was not just any pizza – it was the result of study, research and innovation, all while staying true to tradition.

The first two years were challenging beyond anything we could reasonably have anticipated. Six months after opening, the United Kingdom went into lockdown due to Covid-19. But we held on, continuing with deliveries. The decision to stay open and serve our community during such unprecedented times paid off as it helped us to reach a larger audience. When we reopened the restaurant, many who had ordered from us during lockdown came to dine there and went on to became part of our loyal and regular customer base.

From 2021, accolades began to pour in. The 50 Top Pizza guide listed us among Europe's best pizzerias, awarding us the New Entry prize at 15th place. In 2022, we climbed to 13th. We received two slices from Gambero Rosso. In May 2023, our pizzeria ranked 8th, and I was named Europe's best pizza maker, earning a spot in the world final.

By the end of July 2023, we opened a second location in Richmond, London, as demand had exceeded our capacity of 300–350 pizzas daily, plus a further hundred for take-away.

On 13th September 2023, in the prestigious Royal Palace of Naples, I was announced as the world's best pizza maker. The news was so unexpected that I could hardly believe it. Pushed by a friend, I stood, smiled, went on stage and lifted the trophy with the very same fingers that tentatively kneaded dough to make my first pizza at age 11.

From the next day, Michele Pascarella and Napoli On The Road were featured in top-tier media worldwide. The British press celebrated me as an adopted son, the Italian press as a son who found success far from home, and the international press marvelled at a Neapolitan pizza maker with thriving pizzerias in London. For the next three months we actually had to disconnect our phones due to the overwhelming volume of booking requests! We have since received eye-watering financial offers to establish a chain of pizzerias, but we will continue to decline these simply because it would compromise our pizza's quality. I always tell our customers that it is better to wait a month for a table to be able to come and enjoy our pizza than never to have it again because by turning Napoli on the Road into a chain, it would inevitably become a mass-produced product.

I am proud to share my recipes with you on the following pages and hope you will enjoy making the pizzas as much as I have enjoyed creating them.

MAKING GREAT PIZZA AT HOME

It is possible to make delicious pizza at home. You may not be able to replicate the authentic experience of eating in a pizzeria in a bustling Naples street, or at one of my restaurants, but you will be able to enjoy freshly baked dough with high quality toppings, full of flavour.

using a conventional oven?

At Napoli on the Road our wood-fired oven cooks at 450ºC/840ºF whereas conventional ovens only reach 250ºC/480ºF. As most people making pizza at home will be using this type of oven, my baking method has been devised to allow for this, the aim being to cook the base without drying out the toppings. I give clear instructions in the recipes for cooking each individual pizza and at which stage to add the various toppings, so do refer to these for specific instructions, but here is the basic principle.

Preheating the oven Preheat your oven to the highest temperature it offers for at least 40 minutes. (There is no need to preheat a baking tray/sheet.)

Preparing the pizza base Stretch or roll the pizza dough (see page 15) and place on a heavy baking tray/sheet – this can be the rimmed one that comes with your oven if available, or a round pizza pan.

Adding toppings Add as directed in each recipe.

Initial baking Place the baking tray/sheet with the pizza at the very bottom of your oven, in direct contact with the surface, not on the bottom shelf.

Final baking Once the pizza base is cooked (this will take about 5 minutes, but is dependent on your oven's power), transfer the tray/sheet with the pizza to the upper part of your oven and switch to grill/broil mode. Cook for about 2 minutes, or until the crust is lightly golden. Remove from the oven.

using a pro pizza oven?

If you have invested in an electric, gas or wood-fired pro pizza oven, you will need to follow the method below, which takes the extremely high temperature and thus reduced cooking time into account – almost all models will come with an integral pizza stone. **NOTE** Adding olive oil to pizza dough will help create a browned crust when baking pizza in a conventional oven (see recipe on page 12), but omit if you are using a pro oven as the extreme heat will cause it to reach it's smoke point much faster and start to degrade.

Preheating the oven Preheat your oven to 400ºC/750ºF for at least 30–60 minutes to ensure it reaches the ideal temperature and that the pizza stone is thoroughly heated.

Preparing the pizza base Stretch or roll the pizza dough (see page 15). Transfer the base to a lightly floured pizza peel to prevent sticking.

Adding toppings Evenly distribute your desired toppings on the pizza base, leaving about a 1–2 cm/½ inch border for the crust. (Hold back any toppings that are eaten uncooked, such as rocket/arugula or fresh ham, use these to finish the cooked pizza.)

Transferring the pizza Use the pizza peel to transfer the pizza from the work surface to the hot pizza stone in the oven. Use a quick, jerking motion to slide the pizza onto the stone smoothly.

Baking the pizza Bake the pizza for 2–4 minutes. The very high temperature of the oven allows for rapid and even cooking, resulting in a crispy crust and perfectly melted cheese. Check the pizza frequently. It is done when the crust is golden brown and slightly charred, and the cheese is melted and bubbling. Always use the pizza peel to remove the pizza from the oven and handle with care as it will be extremely hot!

useful equipment

You don't need specialist equipment, simply invest in a few good pieces of kit and you are good to go!

Stand mixer A powerful heavy-based mixer with both whisk and dough hook attachments.

Pizza dough cutter/scraper Used to cut and lift dough, choose one with a handle that is comfortable to hold and has a rounded blade.

Heavy baking tray/sheet See page opposite.

Pizza peel (optional) See page opposite.

Scissors or a pizza wheel cutter I use sharp, long-bladed scissors to cut my pizza into slices as doing so retains the structure of the crust that is unique to Neapolitan pizza. You can use a wheel if you prefer.

Dough container An airtight container is used for proving the dough. Ideally a large lidded box that is at least 10 cm/4 inches deep to allow room for the dough to rise. You will also want it to allow plenty of space between dough balls, because they will spread out as they rest. You should also make sure it fits in your fridge for the Cold Fermentation stage (see page 14).

Digital kitchen scales A good investment generally, but you will get better results if you weigh your dough ingredients, water in particular (see page 12 for Basic Dough), avoid measuring jugs/pitchers that give weight by volume as they are rarely accurate!

Mortar and pestle A great tool for making pesto and other sauces as well as crushing nuts and grinding spices.

Japanese mandoline Ideal for slicing foods such as vegetables very thinly, but use it carefully.

Squeezy bottles These make easy work out of drizzling olive oil or adding sauces and condiments to your pizzas as you assemble them.

a note about ingredients

Flour For the dough, I ideally use an Italian-type 0 flour but 00 flour (also known as *doppio zero*) is fine. It is made from durum wheat and used by 80–90% of the world's pizzerias. If buying other medium strength plain/all-purpose flour, check that the protein content is between 12% and 13%.

Toppings You can buy ready-made sauces and pestos but I strongly recommend that you use my recipes on pages 16–23 for the most delicious and authentic results. However, please be aware that there is simply no substitute for my homemade Neapolitan Ragù (see page 21)!

Cheese Buy the best you can afford (also see note on page 4 on cheeses suitable for vegetarians).

Olive oil Drizzling extra virgin olive oil over your cooked pizza can elevate flavour. Use one with a flavour you enjoy; it's worth tasting before you buy.

making & shaping pizza dough

Making a Neapolitan-style pizza base at home is possible, but care must be taken with both the ingredients and the method for the best results. For best results I use a stand mixer.

basic pizza dough

This recipe makes sufficient dough to create six 32-cm/12-inch diameter pizza bases. If you don't need that number of pizzas, the dough balls can be frozen in a sealed container before the Cold Fermentation stage (see page 14) and then defrosted for a few hours before use.

1 kg/35 oz./7½ cups medium strength flour (see page 11)

700 g/24½ oz. water in total (see page 11)
2 g/scant ½ teaspoon fresh yeast (or 1 g/⅓ teaspoon dry yeast)
25 g/5 teaspoons fine salt
5 g/1 teaspoon extra virgin olive oil (optional, page 12)

a stand mixer with both whisk and dough hook attachments

Initial preparation Tip the flour into the bowl of the stand mixer fitted with the whisk attachment. Add 550 g/19½ oz. of the water to the flour and mix for 3–4 minutes until the mixture is compact [**A, B**].

First resting phase Remove the dough from the mixer and place in a bowl. Cover and leave to rest at room temperature (18–20°C/64–68°F) for 2 hours.

Second mixing phase After the resting period, place the dough back in the bowl of the stand mixer. Dissolve the fresh or dry yeast in 50 g/1¾ oz. water. Add the yeast mixture to the rested dough and start mixing [**C**]. The dough might initially seem a bit loose, but don't worry.

Incorporating the remaining water Gradually add the 100 g/3½ oz. water, in a slow, thin stream, while continuing to mix. When about half of the remaining water has been added, fit the stand mixer with the dough hook and incorporate the salt [**D**]. Continue adding the rest of the water gradually followed by the olive oil (if using, see page 12) until the dough is well combined, smooth and homogeneous [**E**].

Short resting phase Let the dough rest, loosely covered, on the counter for about 20 minutes.

Folding Once rested, perform folding techniques on the dough, turning it onto itself to create a smooth and elastic texture [**F, G, H**].

Bulk fermentation Place the rested and folded dough in a bowl [**I**] tightly covered with cling film/plastic wrap. Leave it to rise for about 3–4 hours at room temperature (18–20°C/64–68°F).

Forming dough balls After 3–4 hours have passed, the dough will have doubled in size [**J**]. Remove the cling film/plastic wrap and tip the dough out from the bowl onto the counter, using a spatula to ease it out [**K**]. Use a dough scraper/cutter to divide into 6 pieces of equal size [**L**]. Use your hands to stretch, fold and shape each piece into a ball [**M**, **N**, **O**].

Resting the dough balls Transfer the dough balls to a suitable lidded container (see page 11), replace the lid and seal. Let the dough balls rest in the container at room temperature for 1–1½ hours.

Cold fermentation After the dough balls have rested, place the sealed container in the fridge at 4–5°C/39–41°F for a further 12–14 hours for cold fermentation to take place.

Preparation for use Remove the container from the fridge and allow a further 30 minutes to 1 hour for the dough to come to room temperature (this will depend on the ambient temperature of your room). Next, use a dough scraper/cutter to carefully remove each ball from the container [**P**] and place it on a floured counter. (You can use wheat or

semolina flour at this point, but do use semolina flour sparingly as too much will taint the taste of your pizza dough once cooked.)

Shaping To shape a dough ball, press it into a disk using your fingers, shaping it so the dough is a little thicker around the outside edge [**Q, R, S**]. Drape it over the back of your hand [**T**] and stretch it over your knuckles. Lift the dough and using both hands use your fists to stretch and turn it until it's about 32 cm/12 inches in diameter [**U**].

Topping and baking your pizza Working quickly, add your chosen toppings and bake as directed by the individual recipes or, if using a pro pizza oven, follow the alternative method given on page 10.

NOTE If you are not confident to shape a base by hand as I do (it takes practice!), you can roll the dough out on a flour-dusted counter using a rolling pin. Do however use a small rolling pin and roll out from the centre of the disk, leaving it thicker around the outside edge to create the delicious risen crust.

SAUCES & CONDIMENTS

slow-cooked tomato sauce

Tomatoes naturally contain lots of water, so if you cook any tomato sauce for a long period of time the water will slowly but surely evaporate, leaving behind a thickened, full-bodied sauce with lots of flavour, which is exactly what this is.

Prepare the tomatoes Bring a large pot of water to the boil. While waiting for the water to boil, make an 'X' incision at the bottom of each tomato. Once the water is boiling, blanch the tomatoes for about 30 seconds or until the skins start to peel away. Transfer the tomatoes to a bowl of iced water to cool. Peel off the skins.

Seeding and chopping Cut the peeled tomatoes in half and remove the seeds. Roughly chop the tomatoes and set them aside.

Cooking the garlic In a large saucepan or pot, heat the extra virgin olive oil over a medium heat. Add the whole garlic clove and sauté until it becomes fragrant and lightly golden, about 2–3 minutes. Be careful not to burn the garlic.

Adding the tomatoes Add the chopped plum tomatoes to the saucepan. Stir to combine with the garlic and oil.

Seasoning Add salt to taste. If the tomatoes are very acidic, add a teaspoon of sugar to balance the flavour. Stir well.

Slow cooking Reduce the heat to low. Let the sauce simmer gently for about 1½–2 hours, stirring occasionally. This slow cooking process will concentrate the flavours and thicken the sauce.

Checking consistency After 1½–2 hours, check the consistency of the sauce. It should be thick and rich. If it's still too watery, continue to simmer until it reaches the desired consistency.

Discarding the garlic Once the sauce is ready, remove the garlic clove to ensure a mild garlic flavour without being overpowering.

Blending If you prefer a smoother sauce, use a stick blender or a regular blender to purée the sauce to your desired texture.

1 kg/2 lb. 4 oz. small fresh plum tomatoes
2 tablespoons extra virgin olive oil
1 garlic clove, peeled and left whole
salt
1 teaspoon sugar (if needed)

MAKES ENOUGH TO TOP 2–3 PIZZAS

basic tomato sauce

This traditional recipe does not include any oil or spices. The simplicity allows the natural flavour of the tomatoes to shine, which makes it the perfect sauce for a pizza base.

1 kg/2 lb. 4 oz. canned whole peeled tomatoes
10 g/2 teaspoons fine salt

MAKES ENOUGH FOR 8–10 PIZZAS

Preparing the tomatoes Pour the tomatoes into a large bowl and crush them with your hands, removing any hard parts or skin residues (this method allows you to maintain a rustic and even texture, preserving the integrity of the pulp and seeds). Alternatively, pass the tomatoes through a food mill – this will separate the seeds and skins while giving you a smooth yet textured sauce.

Add salt Add the salt and mix well to ensure the salt is evenly distributed.

NOTE If possible, avoid using a blender because it can aerate the tomatoes and break down the seeds, making the sauce bitter and overly smooth. The goal is to keep the sauce slightly chunky to retain the natural texture and flavour of the tomatoes.

Keep any leftover sauce for another use or halve the quantities to make less if preferred.

creamy piennolo cherry tomato jam

The Vesuvio Piennolo DOP Cherry Tomato is grown on the slopes of Vesuvius. It has a particularly sweet and intense flavour, making it perfect for a sticky jam/jelly.

500 g/1 lb. 2 oz. Piennolo cherry tomatoes
1 fresh red chilli/chile (optional, for heat)
1 tablespoon olive oil
200 g/1 cup granulated sugar
100 ml/⅓ cup plus 1 tablespoon apple
**   cider vinegar**
1 teaspoon salt
1 teaspoon freshly ground black pepper

MAKES APPROX. 500 ML/16 OZ./2 CUPS

chilli jam

Preparation Wash the Piennolo cherry tomatoes thoroughly and cut them in half. If using, deseed and finely chop the red chilli.

Cooking the tomatoes In a large saucepan, heat the olive oil over a medium heat. Add the cherry tomatoes and the chilli (if using). Stir and cook for about 5 minutes until the tomatoes start to soften.

Adding sugar and vinegar Add the sugar, apple cider vinegar, salt and black pepper to the saucepan. Stir well to combine all the ingredients.

Bringing to the boil Increase the heat for about 5 minutes to dissolve the sugar.

Simmering Reduce the heat to low and let the mixture simmer for about 30–40 minutes. Stir occasionally to prevent sticking. The mixture should thicken and become jam-like, then cook for an additional 2–3 minutes, stirring continuously.

Blending for creaminess For a smoother texture, use a hand-held stick blender directly in the saucepan until you achieve the desired consistency. Alternatively, let the jam cool slightly and blend in a regular blender.

Bottling Allow the jam to cool completely. Using a funnel, transfer the cooled jam into a sterilized squeezy bottle. Seal the bottle tightly.

Storage Store the Piennolo cherry tomato jam in the refrigerator. It should last for up to 3 months.

TIPS

» *Adjust the amount of chilli/chile based on your heat preference.*

» *Ensure the squeezy bottle is thoroughly cleaned and sterilized before use.*

» *Also delicious served with cheese on a cheese platter/board.*

This versatile condiment has a subtle spicy kick and is well worth the effort.

200 g/7 oz. red chillies/chiles, chopped
200 g/7 oz. red (bell) peppers, chopped
2 garlic cloves, chopped
1 piece of fresh ginger (about 5 cm/2 inches), peeled and chopped
500 g/2½ cups granulated sugar
100 ml/⅓ cup plus 1 tablespoon white wine vinegar
1 teaspoon salt

MAKES APPROX 500 ML/16 OZ./2 CUPS

Preparing the ingredients Wash and chop the chillies and red peppers. If you want a milder jam, remove the seeds from the chillies.

Blending Place the chopped chillies, red peppers, garlic and ginger in a food processor. Blend until you have a smooth paste.

Cooking Transfer the chilli paste to a large saucepan. Add the sugar, white wine vinegar and salt. Stir to combine.

Simmering Bring the mixture to the boil over a medium heat, stirring occasionally. Once it starts boiling, reduce the heat to low and simmer for 45–60 minutes, or until it thickens to a jam-like consistency. Stir occasionally to prevent sticking.

Testing To test if the jam is ready, place a small amount on a chilled plate. If it wrinkles when you push it with your finger, it's done. If not, continue simmering and testing every few minutes.

Cooling and storing Once the jam has reached the desired consistency, remove it from the heat and let it cool slightly. Pour the hot chilli jam into sterilized jars and seal them tightly. Let the jars cool completely before storing them in the fridge.

Neapolitan ragù

There are many versions of Neapolitan ragù sauce but this is my grandmother's recipe and one that is very close to my heart. It is traditionally served with ribbons of tagliatelle pasta and grated Parmesan but this is also the essential ingredient for my Ricordi d'Infanzia pizza (see page 134).

Searing the meat Season the beef pieces with salt and pepper. In a large, heavy-bottomed pot, heat the olive oil over a medium-high heat. Add the beef and sear the pieces on all sides until browned. Remove the meat and set aside.

Cooking the onions and garlic In the same pot, add the finely chopped onion and garlic. Cook until the onion becomes translucent and soft, about 5–7 minutes.

Deglazing with wine Pour in the red wine to deglaze the pot, scraping up any browned bits from the bottom. Let the wine simmer until it reduces by half.

Adding the tomatoes Add the tomato purée to the pot, stirring well to combine with the onions and garlic. Then add the passata and stir together well.

Combining meat and sauce Return the browned beef to the pot. Stir to ensure the meat is well-coated with the tomato mixture.

Slow cooking Reduce the heat to low and let the ragù simmer gently, uncovered, for about 6–8 hours, stirring occasionally to prevent sticking. The sauce should thicken and develop a deep, rich flavour. If the sauce becomes too thick, add a bit of water as needed.

Adjusting seasoning Taste the ragù and adjust the seasoning with additional salt and pepper if needed.

Shredding Remove the meat from the sauce and set it on a plate. Using two forks, shred the meat and return it to the sauce.

1 kg/2 lb. 4 oz. beef shank, cut into large pieces
100 ml/⅓ cup plus 1 tablespoon extra virgin olive oil
1 large onion, finely chopped
2 garlic cloves, finely chopped
200 ml/¾ cup red wine
200 g/7 oz. tomato purée/paste
2 litres/8½ cups passata/strained tomatoes
salt and freshly ground black pepper

MAKES ENOUGH TO TOP 8–10 PIZZAS (OR ENJOY WITH TAGLIATELLE AND GRATED PARMESAN)

basil pesto

The traditional sauce – a blend of fresh basil, pine nuts, garlic, Parmesan and olive oil.

1 garlic clove, peeled
30 g/¼ cup pine nuts
50 g/2 oz. fresh basil leaves, washed and patted dry
100 ml/⅓ cup plus 1 tablespoon extra virgin olive oil
30 g/scant ½ cup grated Parmesan
salt and freshly ground black pepper

MAKES ABOUT 160 G/⅔ CUP (TO TOP 2 PIZZAS)

Blending the ingredients Put the garlic clove in a mortar with a little salt and the pine nuts. Pound with a pestle until broken up. Add the basil leaves, a few at a time, pounding and mixing to a paste.

Adding the oil Gradually beat in the extra virgin olive oil, little by little, until the mixture is creamy and thick.

Adding the Parmesan Beat in the grated Parmesan. Adjust the seasoning with salt and freshly ground black pepper to taste. Stir to blend well.

Storage You can use the basil pesto immediately, or store it in the refrigerator in a sealed glass jar (covered with a layer of extra virgin olive oil to exclude the air) for up to one week.

ALTERNATIVELY Place the garlic, basil, pine nuts and Parmesan in a food processor and blend until you get a coarse mixture. Slowly add the extra virgin olive oil while continuing to blend, until you achieve a smooth, creamy consistency. Season and store as above.

pistachio pesto

A twist on a classic pesto recipe, replacing the pine nuts with vibrant green pistachios.

100 g/3½ oz. shelled unsalted pistachios
1 garlic clove, peeled (optional)
10 fresh basil leaves, washed and patted dry
50 ml/3½ tablespoons extra virgin olive oil
30 g/scant ½ cup grated Parmesan
salt and freshly ground black pepper

MAKES ABOUT 160 G/⅔ CUP (TO TOP 2 PIZZAS)

Preparing the pistachios If the pistachios have their skins, blanch them in boiling water for a couple of minutes, then drain and rub between your hands to remove the skins. (This step is optional but will make the pesto a brighter colour.)

Blending the ingredients Put the garlic clove (if using) in a mortar with a little salt and the pistachios. Pound with a pestle until broken up. Add the basil leaves, a few at a time, pounding and mixing to a paste.

Adding the oil Gradually beat in the extra virgin olive oil, little by little, until the mixture is creamy and thick.

Adding the Parmesan Beat in the grated Parmesan. Adjust the seasoning with salt and freshly ground black pepper to taste. Stir to blend well.

ALTERNATIVELY Place the garlic, blanched pistachios and Parmesan in a food processor and blend until you get a coarse mixture. Slowly add the extra virgin olive oil while continuing to blend, until you achieve a smooth, creamy consistency. If the pesto is too thick, add a bit of water (up to 20 ml/4 teaspoons) to achieve the desired consistency. Season and store as above.

Antipasti
APPETIZERS

bruschette

This is a serving suggestion more than a recipe. It features a trio of topped bruschette (crisp toasts), which makes a great appetizer to share. The toasts are made from a loaf baked with pizza dough. You can make as many as you need, and top them as you prefer so I have not specified quantities for the ingredients, simply build the bruschetta by eye. It's best to eat them as soon as possible after making. Feel free to experiment with any other toppings of your choice.

Shaping the dough Remove the dough balls from the fridge and allow 30 minutes to 1 hour for the dough to come to room temperature (this will depend on the ambient temperature of your room). Shape the balls into an oval loaf by folding them together. Allow to rise for a couple of hours.

Preheating the oven Preheat your oven to 180°C/350°F/Gas 4.

Baking the dough Bake the loaf on a baking sheet/tray in the preheated oven for 20–25 minutes, or until it is perfectly cooked.

Slicing the loaf After baking and allowing to cool, use a sharp, serrated knife to cut the loaf into thin slices. Arrange these in a grill pan and toast on both sides under a preheated grill/broiler to create crisp and golden bruschette.

Making the Parmigiano-Reggiano Cream Warm the cream in a small saucepan over a medium heat, being careful not to let it boil. Add the grated Parmigiano-Reggiano to the warm cream, stirring continuously with a whisk to prevent lumps from forming and until the cheese is melted and the cream is smooth and lump-free. Add black pepper to taste and mix well. Set aside until needed.

Adding the toppings For the first bruschetta, top with a few spoonfuls of cherry tomatoes, add some basil leaves, a drizzle of extra virgin olive oil and season with salt and a sprinkle of oregano.

The second is simply made with sliced ripe heirloom tomatoes, Prosciutto and a few rocket leaves.

The third features a luxurious spread made from Parmigiano-Reggiano Cream topped with shiitake mushrooms (that have been previously sautéed in a little olive oil and seasoned with salt and freshly ground black pepper) and shavings of fresh truffle.

---

3 balls pizza dough, after Cold Fermentation (see pages 12–14), which will make a 750-g/26-oz. oval-shaped loaf

PARMIGIANO-REGGIANO CREAM
100 ml/⅓ cup plus 1 tablespoon double/heavy cream
100 g/1½ cups finely grated Parmigiano-Reggiano
freshly ground black pepper

CHERRY TOMATO & BASIL
cherry tomatoes, quartered
fresh basil leaves
extra virgin olive oil, to drizzle
salt and freshly ground black pepper
leaves from a few sprigs of fresh oregano (or a pinch of dried), to finish

TOMATO, PROSCIUTTO & ROCKET/ARUGULA
ripe heirloom tomatoes, thinly sliced
sliced Prosciutto
rocket/arugula

PARMIGIANO-REGGIANO CREAM & MUSHROOM WITH TRUFFLE
Parmigiano-Reggiano Cream (see above)
shiitake mushrooms, sliced
fresh truffle, to shave
extra virgin olive oil, to sauté

crocchè di patate

These potato croquettes are a delightful treat, perfect as an appetizer or a snack. Enjoy cooking and sharing them.

Boiling the potatoes Start by washing the potatoes thoroughly (do not peel them). Boil them in a pot of salted water until they are completely tender, which usually takes about 20–30 minutes depending on the size. Once done, drain and let them cool slightly.

Preparing the potato mixture Peel the potatoes while they are still warm and mash them using a potato masher or pass them through a potato ricer. Ensure there are no lumps. Allow the mashed potatoes to cool to room temperature, then add the beaten egg, grated Parmesan, chopped parsley, salt and freshly ground black pepper. Mix well until all ingredients are thoroughly combined.

Shaping the crocchè Take a portion of the potato mixture (about 100 g/3½ oz. – the size of a small potato) and flatten it slightly in the palm of your hand. Place a few cubes of mozzarella in the centre, then fold the potato mixture around the cheese to form an oval or cylindrical shape. Ensure the cheese is completely enclosed to prevent it leaking out during frying.

Coating the crocchè Place the flour, beaten eggs and breadcrumbs in three separate shallow bowls. Roll each crocchè first in the flour, then dip it into the beaten eggs, and finally, coat it well with breadcrumbs. Make sure each crocchè is completely covered in breadcrumbs for a crisp finish.

Frying the crocchè Heat a generous amount of oil in a deep fat fryer or a deep frying pan/skillet to 170°C (340°F). Fry the crocchè in batches, without overcrowding the pan, until they are golden brown and crispy, about 4–5 minutes. Remove the crocchè with a slotted spoon and drain on paper towels to remove excess oil.

Serving Serve the crocchè hot and crispy, ideally fresh out of the fryer for the best texture and taste. Serve with a small bowl of Parmigiano-Reggiano Cream for dipping, if liked.

1.2 kg/2¾ lb. potatoes (preferably starchy type)
1 egg, beaten
80 g/1¼ cups finely grated Parmesan
leaves from a small bunch of flat-leaf parsley, finely chopped
200 g/7 oz. mozzarella cheese, cut into small cubes
sunflower oil, sufficient for deep frying
salt and freshly ground black pepper
Parmigiano-Reggiano Cream, to serve (optional, see page 26)

FOR COATING
150 g/1 cup plus 2 tablespoons plain/all-purpose flour
2 eggs, beaten
200 g/2 cups dried breadcrumbs, such as panko

MAKES 8

arancini al ragù

Arancini translates as 'little orange', which explains the size and colour of these filled rice balls. The rich meat ragù filling with peas and Parmesan is a classic and much loved all over Italy, especially in the South.

Preparing the sauce Heat the olive oil in a large frying pan/skillet over a medium heat. Add the chopped onions and cook until translucent. Add the minced beef, breaking it up with a spoon, and cook until browned. Stir in the tomato sauce and peas (if using). Season with salt and pepper. Simmer the sauce for about 20 minutes until thickened. Set aside to cool.

Cooking the rice In a large pot, heat a splash of olive oil over a medium heat. Add the rice and toast it lightly for 2–3 minutes. Gradually add the vegetable stock, stirring continuously, and cook for 15–20 minutes until the rice is fully cooked and creamy. Remove from the heat. Stir in the grated Parmigiano-Reggiano. Season with salt and pepper to taste. Allow the rice to cool to room temperature, then chill in the fridge until completely cold.

Forming the arancini Take about 60 g/½ cup of the cooled rice and flatten it on your palm. Place a small spoonful of the meat sauce and a few pieces of diced mozzarella in the centre. Enclose the filling with the rice, forming a tightly packed ball. Repeat this process until all ingredients are used up. The trick is to mould the rice carefully in your cupped hand to create a hollow that holds as much ragù as possible and then close the mould carefully, shaping as if you were cradling a ball. Once shaped and crumbed, it can be kept for up to 2 days in the fridge before frying.

Coating the arancini Place the flour, beaten eggs and breadcrumbs in three separate shallow bowls. Roll each rice ball first in flour, then dip in beaten eggs, and finally coat with breadcrumbs.

Frying the arancini Heat the vegetable oil in a deep fat fryer or a deep frying pan/skillet to 180°C (350°F). Fry the arancini in batches for 4–5 minutes until golden brown and heated through. Remove the arancini with a slotted spoon and drain on paper towels to remove excess oil. These are best served hot with a tomato sauce on the side and an Italian leaf salad, if liked.

45 ml/3 tablespoons olive oil
1–2 onions, finely chopped (about 225 g/2 cups once chopped)
450 g/2 cups minced/ground beef
360 ml/1½ cups Basic Tomato Sauce (see page 18)
125 g/1 cup peas, fresh or frozen (optional)
600 g/3 cups Arborio (risotto) rice
1.5 litres/6 cups vegetable stock/ broth
75 g/1 cup finely grated Parmigiano-Reggiano
150 g/6 oz. mozzarella, diced
plain/all-purpose flour, for coating (about 100 g/¾ cup)
3 large eggs, beaten (about 150 ml/⅔ cup)
300 g/3 cups dried breadcrumbs, such as panko
sunflower oil, sufficient for deep frying
salt and freshly ground black pepper

TO SERVE
Slow-cooked Tomato Sauce, to serve (see page 16)
Italian leaf salad (optional)

MAKES 10–12 ARANCINI

frittatine di pasta

Frittatine di pasta are a common sight in the streets of Naples. They are balls or slices of cheesy pasta, which have been battered, breaded and fried to perfection. With a crispy, crunchy shell and a gooey inside, these street food treats are worth trying at least once.

Cooking the pasta Boil a large pot of salted water and cook the pasta until al dente. Drain and rinse under cold water to stop the cooking process. Set aside.

Making the béchamel sauce In a saucepan, melt the butter over a medium heat. Add the flour and whisk until smooth to create a roux. Gradually pour in the milk, while stirring continuously to avoid lumps. Add a pinch of nutmeg and salt to taste. Keep stirring until the mixture thickens into a creamy béchamel sauce.

Combining ingredients In a large bowl, mix the cooled pasta with the béchamel sauce, ensuring the pasta is well coated. Stir in the diced ham, grated Parmesan and Pecorino Romano. Season with salt and pepper to taste.

Forming the pasta balls Weigh out about 120 g/4¼ oz. of the pasta mixture for each ball. Shape them into firm, round balls.

Preparing the batter In a shallow bowl, mix the flour and 100 g/ 3½ oz. water to make a batter similar in consistency to a thin pancake batter. Dip each pasta ball into the batter, ensuring they are evenly coated.

Frying Heat the oil in a deep fat fryer or a large deep frying pan/ skillet to 180°C (350°F). Carefully place the coated pasta balls in the hot oil and fry for about 2 minutes or until golden brown and crispy. Remove the frittatine with a slotted spoon and drain on paper towels to remove excess oil.

Serving Serve the fried pasta balls hot, with a side of Parmigiano-Reggiano Cream for dipping, if liked.

500 g/1 lb. 2 oz. dried bucatini pasta*
200 g/7 oz. cooked ham, diced
100 g/1½ cups finely grated Parmesan
50 g/¾ cup finely grated Pecorino Romano
70–80 g/½ cup plain/all-purpose flour, for the batter
salt and freshly ground black pepper
sunflower oil, sufficient for deep frying

BÉCHAMEL SAUCE
100 g/7 tablespoons butter
100 g/¾ cup plain/all-purpose flour
1 litre/4 cups whole/full-fat milk
a pinch of nutmeg

TO SERVE
Parmigiano-Reggiano Cream (optional, see page 26)

MAKES 10–15

* A thick spaghetti-like pasta with a hole running through the middle.

insalata di burrata e pomodorini

Burrata cheese is a variation of classic mozzarella that is stuffed with a filling made of cream and small curds of mozzarella, reminiscent of soft butter, *burro* in Italian, hence 'burrata'. Enjoy the simplicity and freshness of each bite!

Preparing the cheese Leave the burrata cheese at room temperature for about 15–20 minutes. This allows the cheese to become creamy and soft inside.

Plating the salad Place the burrata on a serving plate over a bed of rocket. Scatter a handful of tomatoes around the cheese. Drizzle with olive oil and balsamic vinegar, if liked, then season with a pinch of salt to taste.

Serving Serve this delightfully simple salad with slices of toasted bread, perfect for scooping up the creamy burrata and the flavourful dressing.

100–150 g/3½–5½ oz. ball
  of burrata
a handful of rocket/arugula
a handful of cherry tomatoes
  in different colours, halved
extra virgin olive oil
aged balsamic vinegar (optional)
salt
sliced and toasted bread,
  to serve (see page 26)

SERVES 1–2

arancini
cacio e pepe

Cacio e pepe is a classic Italian pasta dish made with the simplest of ingredients, including Pecorino Romano and freshly ground black pepper (see my Cacio e Pepe inspired pizza on page 56). This recipe merges arancini with the rich flavours of cacio e pepe, to create a delicious twist on the classic Sicilian snack.

Cooking the rice In a large pot, heat the olive oil over a medium heat. Add the rice and toast it lightly for 2–3 minutes. Gradually add the vegetable stock, stirring continuously for about 15–20 minutes until the rice is fully cooked and creamy. Remove from the heat and set aside.

Making the béchamel sauce In a saucepan, melt the butter over a medium heat. Stir in the flour and cook for about 2 minutes to make a roux. Gradually whisk in the milk, ensuring there are no lumps. Cook, stirring continuously, until the sauce thickens. Remove from the heat, stir in the grated cheeses and freshly ground black pepper. Adjust the seasoning with more pepper if desired and add salt to taste.

Combining the rice with the sauce Mix the cooked rice with the béchamel sauce until well combined. The mixture should be creamy and thick. Allow the rice mixture to cool to room temperature, then cover and refrigerate until completely cold.

Forming the arancini Once the rice mixture is cold, take about 60 g/½ cup of mixture and form it into an oval or cylindrical shape. Repeat this process until all the rice mixture is used.

Coating the arancini Place the flour, beaten eggs and breadcrumbs in three separate shallow bowls. Roll each rice ball first in flour, then dip in beaten eggs, and finally coat with breadcrumbs.

Frying the arancini Heat the vegetable oil in a deep fat fryer or a large, deep frying pan/skillet to 180°C (350°F). Fry the arancini in batches for 4–5 minutes until golden brown and heated through. Remove the arancini with a slotted spoon and drain on paper towels to remove excess oil.

Serving Serve the arancini hot, with a litte extra grated Pecorino Romano on the side for sprinkling.

45 ml/3 tablespoons olive oil
600 g/3 cups arborio (risotto) rice
1.5 litres/6 cups vegetable stock/
    broth
plain/all-purpose flour, for coating
    (about 100g/¾ cup)
3 UK large/US extra large eggs,
    beaten (about 150 g/⅔ cup)
300 g/3 cups dried breadcrumbs,
    such as panko
sunflower oil, sufficient for
    deep frying

BÉCHAMEL SAUCE
30 g/2 tablespoons butter
30 g/¼ cup plain/all-purpose flour
475 ml/2 scant cups whole/full-fat
    milk
100 g/1 heaping cup finely grated
    Pecorino Romano, plus extra
    to serve
50 g/¾ cup finely grated
    Parmigiano-Reggiano
1 teaspoon freshly ground black
    pepper, or more to taste
salt

MAKES 10–12 ARANCINI

pizze fritti

Pizze fritti are buns made by frying pizza dough in oil. The dough puffs up as it cooks so the resulting bun is chewy on the inside and crisp on the outside. It's a great way to use any leftover pizza dough or some you may have stored in the freezer. Here I've filled mine with Neapolitan Ragù (see page 21), but feel free to go with any fillings of your choice or simply serve them alongside antipasti as an accompaniment to cheese, cured meats and olives on a sharing board.

1 ball pizza dough, after Cold Fermentation (see pages 12–14)
sunflower oil, sufficient for deep frying

TO SERVE AS SHOWN (OPTIONAL)
Neapolitan Ragù (see page 21)
finely grated Parmesan
freshly ground black pepper

MAKES 3 ROLLS READY TO FILL

Preparing the dough Divide the pizza dough into three pieces and shape each portion into a small ball. Allow the balls to rest for 1–1½ hours. When ready, gently flatten each ball with your hand to form a round shape, but not too large or thin, about 2.5 cm/1 inch thick (not any thinner).

Frying the buns Heat the oil in a deep fat fryer or large heavy based frying pan/skillet to 180°C (350°F). Fry the dough rounds for about 3–4 minutes until they are uniformly golden and crispy on both sides. Drain on paper towels to remove excess oil.

Serving Once fried, allow to cool slightly then split each bun in half using a sharp serrated knife. Serve hot with the filling of your choice.

Le pizze classiche

CLASSIC PIZZAS

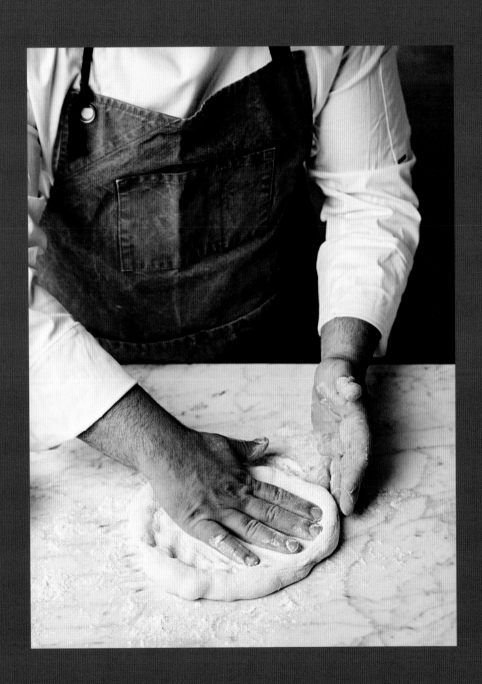

A cornerstone of tradition

Pizza is universally regarded as an Italian product, but here's a surprising fact: Italian cuisine, as a singular entity, doesn't actually exist. The term 'Italian cuisine' refers to the diverse regional cuisines of the Italian peninsula, which share common elements like pasta, tomatoes, extra virgin olive oil and Parmesan. However, there are also distinct differences at regional and even city level. This local diversity is a result of Italy being one of the last European countries to unify, leading to deep cultural, linguistic and culinary variations that persist to this day.

If you've enjoyed pizza in Venice or Florence and found it crispy, you should know that this is not Neapolitan pizza. Neapolitan pizza is a distinct product: round, soft and easily digestible. Other regions in Italy have their own types of pizza, but these are different products entirely. Neapolitan pizza is steeped in tradition, but my pizza aims to innovate while staying true to its roots. This is why we are dedicated to experimentation and the creation of new pizzas at Napoli on the Road. My pizza dough contains almost 80 per cent water, compared to the traditional average of less than 60 per cent. Such a dough cannot cook at 500ºC (930ºF) like most traditional pizzas; it would burn. Instead, it cooks at 380–390ºC (715–735ºF) for about two minutes, allowing the water to evaporate slowly.

It takes a team of four to make each of our pizzas. One rolls out the dough, another adds the toppings, a third bakes the pizza and the last person ensures it meets our quality standards before adding the finishing touches. This process is the reason why our menu features a limited selection of 12–14 pizzas; it also allows us to offer only the highest quality ingredients, many of which are imported from Italy. One section of our menu includes classic pizzas like Margherita, Marinara and Capricciosa, which we offer year-round. The other section changes every three months to reflect seasonal ingredients. We were the first in London to regularly update our menu; a practice that has now become common.

The Margherita is the queen of pizzas. It is made with San Marzano tomatoes, fior di latte, extra virgin olive oil, 36-month aged Parmigiano-Reggiano and basil. According to a widely told but debated legend, the Margherita was named after Queen Margherita of Savoy, who in 1889 chose this pizza from three created by the Neapolitan pizzaiolo Raffaele Esposito.

The white fior di latte, red tomato and green basil were said to represent the colours of the Italian flag. Regardless of the legend's accuracy, the Margherita is a timeless classic, the pizza most commonly eaten in Naples and the first any pizzaiolo learns to make. The Margherita also perfectly embodies the excellence of Campania, the region with Naples as its capital. From the elongated San Marzano DOP tomato, ideal for quick cooking due to its low water content and few seeds, to the extra virgin olive oil and the soft, flavourful fior di latte, each ingredient is carefully selected.

Classic pizzas, especially abroad, serve as a flagship for communicating the culture behind Neapolitan pizza. However, I also strive to incorporate unique touches. For example, in our Provola e Pepe, I use four different types of pepper: white Sarawak, red and black Kampot and Tellicherry. These Asian and Indian peppers, with their intense or subtle flavours and fruity or woody aromas, complement the flavour of provola, another Campanian product of exceptional quality.

My Capricciosa Bianca stays true to the traditional ingredients of ham, mushrooms, olives and artichokes, but with a twist. I add fresh Big Storico ham after cooking to preserve its quality and flavour. I also use Japanese shiitake mushrooms for their earthy, slightly spicy and sweet taste. My Capricciosa Bianca is also a white pizza, made without tomato, to highlight the individual flavours of these ingredients.

My classic pizzas in this chapter are designed to communicate my deep connection to the traditions of a product rooted in my cultural heritage, while remaining open to the influences of global flavours. They have profoundly influenced my own journey in the world of pizza-making. These are the pizzas I have cherished since childhood, carrying their flavours with me over the years. No matter where you go in the world, a true Italian pizzeria will offer these timeless recipes. They evoke a sense of home for Italians abroad and bring back memories for anyone who has enjoyed pizza in Italy. These classic Neapolitan pizzas are a cornerstone of tradition, bridging our past and future in the world of pizza.

margherita

A timeless classic with fresh tomatoes, fior di latte and basil.

Preheating the oven Preheat your oven to its highest temperature for at least 40 minutes.

Preparing the pizza base Begin with dough that has been allowed to rise properly. Roll out the dough ball on a lightly floured surface, forming a slightly raised edge around the sides (see page 15). Lift onto a baking sheet.

Adding the tomato Evenly spread the passata over the pizza base, avoiding the edges. Season with a pinch of salt.

Initial baking Place the pizza at the bottom of the preheated oven (see page 10) and bake for about 5 minutes.

Adding the cheeses After the initial 5 minutes of baking, when the base is nearly but not fully cooked, remove the pizza from the oven. Add the pieces of fior di latte and sprinkle with Parmigiano-Reggiano.

Final baking Transfer the pizza to the upper part of the oven and switch to the grill/broil mode. Cook for about 2 minutes, or until the cheese has melted and the crust is lightly golden.

Finishing and serving Remove the pizza from the oven and garnish with fresh basil leaves and a final drizzle of extra virgin olive oil. Let the pizza rest for a minute before slicing and serving.

1 ball Pizza Dough (see pages 12–15)
flour, for dusting
90 g/⅓ cup passata/strained tomatoes
70 g/2½ oz. fior di latte, torn into pieces
10 g/1½ tablespoons finely grated Parmigiano-Reggiano
a few fresh basil leaves
extra virgin olive oil, to drizzle
salt

carbonara

Creamy indulgence with guanciale (Italian cured pork), eggs and a touch of freshly ground black pepper.

Preheating the oven Preheat your oven to its highest temperature for at least 40 minutes.

Preparing the topping Cut the guanciale into small pieces, place in a small frying pan/skillet and cook over a gentle heat until crispy.

Making the sauce Place the egg yolks and 20 g/3 tablespoons of the grated Pecorino Romano in a heatproof bowl. Place over a pan of gently simmering water (or use a bain marie) and heat for a few minutes, stirring, until it becomes a creamy sauce.

Preparing the pizza base Begin with dough that has been allowed to rise properly. Roll out the dough ball on a lightly floured surface, forming a slightly raised edge around the sides (see page 15). Lift onto a baking sheet.

Adding the toppings Evenly spread the fior di latte and crispy guanciale over the pizza base, and add a drizzle of extra virgin olive oil.

Initial baking Place the pizza at the bottom of the preheated oven (see page 10) and bake for about 5 minutes.

Final baking Transfer the pizza to the upper part of the oven and switch to the grill/broil mode. Cook for about 2 minutes, or until the cheese has melted and the crust is lightly golden.

Finishing and serving Remove the pizza from the oven and drizzle over the egg yolk cream, the rest of the Pecorino Romano, a grating of black pepper and a final drizzle of extra virgin olive oil. Let the pizza rest for a minute before slicing and serving.

1 ball Pizza Dough (see pages 12–15)
100 g/3½ oz. guanciale (Italian cured pork)
2 egg yolks
50 g/⅔ cup grated Pecorino Romano
flour, for dusting
100 g/3½ oz. fior di latte, torn into pieces
extra virgin olive oil, to drizzle
freshly ground black pepper

La Romana

A Roman specialty with anchovies, oregano and mozzarella.

Preheating the oven Preheat your oven to its highest temperature for at least 40 minutes.

Preparing the pizza base Begin with dough that has been allowed to rise properly. Roll out the dough ball on a lightly floured surface, forming a slightly raised edge around the sides (see page 15). Lift onto a baking sheet.

Adding ingredients Evenly spread the tomato sauce over the pizza base, avoiding the edges. Season with a pinch of salt.

Initial baking Place the pizza at the bottom of the preheated oven (see page 10) and bake for about 5 minutes.

Adding the cheeses After the initial 5 minutes of baking, when the base is nearly but not fully cooked, remove the pizza from the oven. Add the pieces of fior di latte.

Final baking Transfer the pizza to the upper part of the oven and switch to the grill/broil mode. Cook for about 2 minutes, or until the cheese is melted and the crust is lightly golden.

Finishing and serving Remove the pizza from the oven, and garnish with anchovies, fresh basil leaves, oregano and a drizzle of extra virgin olive oil. Let the pizza rest for a minute before slicing and serving.

1 ball Pizza Dough (see pages 12–15)
flour, for dusting
100 g/3½ oz. Basic Tomato Sauce
   (see page 18)
80 g/2¾ oz. fior di latte,
   torn into pieces
6 canned anchovy fillets
a few fresh basil leaves
dried oregano, for sprinkling
extra virgin olive oil, to drizzle
salt

capricciosa bianca

A rich combination of ham, salami, mushrooms, chargrilled artichokes and black olives.

Preheating the oven Preheat your oven to its highest temperature for at least 40 minutes.

Preparing the pizza base Begin with dough that has been allowed to rise properly. Roll out the dough ball on a lightly floured surface, forming a slightly raised edge around the sides (see page 15). Lift onto a baking sheet.

Adding the toppings Evenly spread the fior di latte over the pizza base, avoiding the edges. Season with a pinch of salt, then add the mushrooms, black olives, salami Napoli and chargrilled artichokes.

Initial baking Place the pizza at the bottom of the preheated oven (see page 10) and bake for about 5 minutes. Remove the pizza from the oven and sprinkle with the Parmigiano Reggiano.

Final baking Transfer the pizza to the upper part of the oven and switch to the grill/broil mode and cook for about 2 minutes, or until the crust is lightly golden.

Finishing and serving Remove the pizza from the oven, add the fresh ham, basil, a grinding of black pepper and a drizzle of extra virgin olive oil. Let the pizza rest for a minute before slicing and serving.

1 ball Pizza Dough (see pages 12–15)
flour, for dusting
100 g/3½ oz. fior di latte, torn into pieces
30 g/1 oz. shiitake mushrooms
15 g/½ oz. stoned/pitted black olives
40 g/1½ oz. salami Napoli, cut into small strips
30 g/1 oz. chargrilled artichokes in oil (antipasti style), sliced
10 g/1½ tablespoons finely grated Parmigiano-Reggiano
70 g/2½ oz. prime quality fresh ham, cut or torn into strips
a few fresh basil leaves
extra virgin olive oil, to drizzle
salt and freshly ground black pepper

'we're on fire'

Fiery and creamy with rich tomato, 'nduja (spreadable spicy pork sausage from Calabria) and buffalo stracciatella.

Preheating the oven Preheat your oven to its highest temperature for at least 40 minutes.

Preparing the pizza base Begin with dough that has been allowed to rise properly. Roll out the dough ball on a lightly floured surface, forming a slightly raised edge around the sides (see page 15). Lift onto a baking sheet.

Adding the tomato Evenly spread the passata over the pizza base, avoiding the edges. Season with a pinch of salt.

Initial baking Place the pizza at the bottom of the preheated oven (see page 10) and bake for about 5 minutes.

Adding more toppings After the initial 5 minutes of baking, when the base is nearly but not fully cooked, remove the pizza from the oven. Add dollops of 'nduja over the top and sprinkle with the Parmigiano-Reggiano.

Final baking Transfer the pizza to the upper part of the oven and switch to the grill/broil mode. Cook for about 2 minutes, or until the crust is lightly golden.

Finishing and serving Remove the pizza from the oven, add the stracciatella, basil leaves and a drizzle of extra virgin olive oil. Let the pizza rest for a minute before slicing and serving.

1 ball Pizza Dough (see pages 12–15)
flour, for dusting
120 g/⅓ cup passata/strained tomatoes
100 g/3½ oz. 'nduja
10 g/1½ tablespoons finely grated Parmigiano-Reggiano
80 g/3 oz. stracciatella
a few fresh basil leaves
extra virgin olive oil, to drizzle
salt

cacio e pepe

A creamy and peppery Roman classic.

1 ball Pizza Dough (see pages 12–15)
flour, for dusting
100 ml/⅓ cup plus 1 tablespoon double/heavy cream
60 g/heaping ⅔ cup finely grated Pecorino Romano
40 g/scant ⅔ cup finely grated Parmesan
80 g/2¾ oz. fior di latte, torn into pieces
freshly ground black pepper
extra virgin olive oil, to drizzle
balsamic glaze, to drizzle

Preheating the oven Preheat your oven to its highest temperature for at least 40 minutes.

Preparing the pizza base Begin with dough that has been allowed to rise properly. Roll out the dough ball on a lightly floured surface, forming a slightly raised edge around the sides (see page 15). Lift onto a baking sheet.

Making the cacio e pepe cream In a pan, heat the cream over a medium heat, being careful not to bring it to the boil. Add the grated cheeses, stirring continuously with a whisk until the cheese has completely melted and the cream is smooth. Add black pepper to taste and mix well. Evenly spread the cream over the pizza base, avoiding the edges.

Initial baking Place the pizza at the bottom of the oven (see page 10) and bake for about 5 minutes.

Adding the cheese Remove the pizza from the oven and add the pieces of fior di latte.

Final baking Transfer the pizza to the upper part of the oven and switch to the grill/broil mode. Cook for about 2 minutes, or until the cheese has melted and the crust is lightly golden.

Finishing and serving Remove the pizza from the oven and add a sprinkle of black pepper and a drizzle of balsamic glaze. Let the pizza rest for a minute before slicing and serving.

prosciutto e fungi

A classic pairing of ham and mushrooms.

1 ball Pizza Dough (see pages 12–15)
flour, for dusting
90 g/⅓ cup passata/strained tomatoes
100 g/4 oz. prime quality fresh ham, torn into pieces
40 g/1½ oz. mushrooms, sliced and sautéed in a little oil until golden
70 g/2½ oz. fior di latte, torn into pieces
10 g/1½ tablespoons grated Parmigiano-Reggiano
a few fresh basil leaves
extra virgin olive oil, to sauté and drizzle
salt

Preheating the oven Preheat your oven to its highest temperature for at least 40 minutes.

Preparing the pizza base Begin with dough that has been allowed to rise properly. Roll out the dough ball on a lightly floured surface, forming a slightly raised edge around the sides (see page 15). Lift onto a baking sheet.

Adding the toppings Evenly spread the passata over the pizza base, avoiding the edges. Season with a pinch of salt and add the ham and sautéed mushrooms.

Initial baking Place the pizza at the bottom of the oven (see page 10) and bake for about 5 minutes.

Adding the cheeses Remove the pizza from the oven. Add the pieces of fior di latte and sprinkle with Parmigiano-Reggiano.

Final baking Transfer the pizza to the upper part of the oven and switch to the grill/broil mode. Cook for about 2 minutes, or until the cheese has melted and the crust is lightly golden.

Finishing and serving Remove the pizza from the oven and garnish with fresh basil and a drizzle of extra virgin olive oil. Let the pizza rest for a minute before slicing and serving.

diavolo

A spicy crowd-pleasing favourite with hot salami.

Preheating the oven Preheat your oven to its highest temperature for at least 40 minutes.

Preparing the pizza base Begin with dough that has been allowed to rise properly. Roll out the dough ball on a lightly floured surface, forming a slightly raised edge around the sides (see page 15). Lift onto a baking sheet.

Adding the toppings Evenly spread the passata over the pizza base, avoiding the edges. Season with a pinch of salt and add the salami.

Initial baking Place the pizza at the bottom of the preheated oven (see page 10) and bake for about 5 minutes.

Adding the cheeses After the initial 5 minutes of baking, when the base is nearly but not fully cooked, remove the pizza from the oven. Add the pieces of fior di latte and sprinkle with the Parmigiano Reggiano.

Final baking Transfer the pizza to the upper part of the oven and switch to the grill/broil mode. Cook for about 2 minutes, or until the cheese has melted and the crust is lightly golden.

Finishing and serving Remove the pizza from the oven and garnish with fresh basil leaves and a drizzle of extra virgin olive oil. Let the pizza rest for a minute before slicing and serving.

1 ball Pizza Dough (see pages 12–15)
flour, for dusting
90 g/⅓ cup passata/strained tomatoes
100 g/3½ oz. spicy salami, sliced
70 g/2½ oz. fior di latte, torn into pieces
10 g/1½ tablespoons grated Parmigiano-Reggiano
a few fresh basil leaves
extra virgin olive oil, to drizzle
salt

ripieno al forno

A hearty baked calzone (a sealed pizza parcel) filled with rich and savoury ingredients.

Preheating the oven Preheat your oven to its highest temperature for at least 40 minutes.

Preparing the pizza base Begin with dough that has been allowed to rise properly. Roll out the dough ball on a lightly floured surface, forming a slightly raised edge around the sides (see page 15). Lift onto baking sheet.

Adding the base layer Spread a layer of ricotta evenly on the base of the dough.

Add the toppings Top the ricotta with two-thirds of the tomato sauce, the sliced salami Napoli, two-thirds of the fior di latte, a sprinkle of grated Parmesan, a drizzle of olive oil and a grating of black pepper.

Folding the dough Fold the dough over itself to enclose the filling, creating a folded pizza or calzone. Make sure to seal the edges well by pressing them together.

Making a vent Create a small hole on the top of the dough to allow steam to escape.

Adding more toppings Place the remaining tomato sauce and fior di latte on top of the calzone to prevent the dough from burning.

Baking Bake at the bottom of the preheated oven for 6–7 minutes until the dough is golden brown and the cheese is melted and bubbly on top.

Finishing and serving Remove the pizza from the oven and garnish with fresh basil leaves. Let the pizza rest for a minute before slicing and serving.

1 ball Pizza Dough (see pages 12–15)
flour, for dusting
60 g/2¼ oz. ricotta
80 g/2¾ oz. Basic Tomato Sauce (see page 18)
80 g/2¾ oz. salami Napoli, cut into very fine strips
80 g/2¾ oz. fior di latte, torn into pieces
1½ tablespoons finely grated Parmesan
extra virgin olive oil, to drizzle
a few fresh basil leaves
freshly ground black pepper

salame piccante e marmellata di peperoncini

A spicy delight with pepperoni and a homemade sticky and sweet chilli jam.

Preheating the oven Preheat your oven to its highest temperature for at least 40 minutes.

Preparing the pizza base Begin with dough that has been allowed to rise properly. Roll out the dough ball on a lightly floured surface, forming a slightly raised edge around the sides (see page 15). Lift onto a baking sheet.

Adding the toppings Evenly spread the passata over the pizza base, avoiding the edges. Season with a pinch of salt and add the chorizo.

Initial baking Place the pizza at the bottom of the preheated oven (see page 10) and bake for about 5 minutes.

Adding the cheeses After the initial 5 minutes of baking, when the base is nearly but not fully cooked, remove the pizza from the oven. Add the pieces of fior di latte and sprinkle with the Parmigiano-Reggiano.

Final baking Transfer the pizza to the upper part of the oven and switch to the grill/broil mode. Cook for about 2 minutes, or until the cheese has melted and the crust is lightly golden.

Finishing and serving Remove the pizza from the oven, scatter over the chopped parsley, add small dollops of the Chilli Jam and a drizzle of extra virgin olive oil. Let the pizza rest for a minute before slicing and serving.

1 ball Pizza Dough (see pages 12–15)
flour, for dusting
90 g/⅓ cup passata/strained tomatoes
100 g/4 oz. chorizo, sliced
70 g/2½ oz. fior di latte, torn into pieces
1½ tablespoons finely grated Parmigiano-Reggiano
1 tablespoon freshly chopped flat-leaf parsley
30 g/1½ tablespoons Chilli Jam (see page 19)
extra virgin olive oil, to drizzle
salt

Primavera
SPRING

a change in the air

It happens suddenly. One day you're still bundled up against the cold, and then a gentle breeze lets you know that spring is coming. In Italy, the transition is more distinct, especially in the south. But even in a climatically bizarre country like England, where the four seasons can appear all together in one (theoretically) summer day, the scent of spring is unmistakable. It's a moment, a sensation so fleeting yet easy to grasp because you know winter is ending. What better way to celebrate the arrival of spring than with a well-made pizza?

In the kitchen, too, the arrival of spring brings with it a riot of colours. Tomatoes, asparagus, peas, artichokes, new potatoes, radishes. Ah, the many delicious things this time of year brings, along with new challenges to create pairings never dared before.

In late spring, aubergines (eggplants) also arrive. We serve Parmigiana, but please don't ask for it in winter – there are no aubergines in winter. It would taste unnatural, and I want you to eat only an excellent pizza if I make that pizza. To allow my staff to answer customers with maximum clarity when they ask us 'everyone else has Parmigiana, why don't you?', I took them all to Italy at the beginning of one spring.

We closed the restaurant for five days and flew to Naples. My staff isn't just made up of Neapolitans but also Italians from other regions and others are different nationalities. I wanted all of them to really understand what we serve to our customers every day. A 'full immersion' training so that each of them would know where and how the buffalo mozzarella is made, how the flour we use is produced, where we get our extra virgin olive oil and wine, but especially what grows and is harvested in the fields.

Today, each of us uses objects we wouldn't know how to produce nor know how they are made. And even with food, we have become increasingly used to seeing it on supermarket shelves or directly on the

plate in restaurants. But where does it come from? How are the ingredients produced? In what season are vegetables harvested? Olive oil comes from the fruit of a tree called the olive, not from a glass bottle. Similarly, wine is born from grapes growing on vines, and the aubergine is a plant that is cultivated. I consider it essential that my staff has at least basic knowledge to correctly explain that seasonality is a cornerstone of food culture. And only by involving my team can I pass this knowledge to those who come to the restaurant to eat my pizza.

In spring, we also offer a section of the menu that is exclusively seasonal. Peas are one of the symbols of spring and are typical of Neapolitan cuisine. Cultivated for thousands of years and originating from the Middle East, they probably arrived on the southern Italian coasts with Greek colonists. (In fact, Naples was founded as a Greek colony, and the city's name derives from the Greek *nea polis* which simply means new city.)

One of the most famous Neapolitan dishes is pasta and peas. For my pea pizza, I use a pea cream topped with the savoury contrast of high-quality cooked ham. Contrast is one of the key elements of good cuisine and also provides the lesson that the pairing of differences creates the best result. Not

surprisingly, although belonging to the Neapolitan pizza-making tradition, which has a very distinct identity, I do not hesitate to use ingredients from other Italian regions or other countries.

My aspiration is to make pizzas that tell and intertwine the flavours of the world. 'Nduja, for example, is a spreadable sausage typical of Calabria, another southern Italian region, and characterized by its extreme spiciness. On my pizza I pair it with the sweet and intense flavour of yellow cherry tomatoes and the aroma of fresh basil. Or my pizza with pesto, the famous sauce predominantly produced in Liguria and Sicily, derived from a preparation already present in ancient Rome, paired with sweet red cherry tomatoes. Or again, the pizza with a Jerusalem artichoke cream (which, despite its name, is not an artichoke) as a base, and grilled artichokes as a topping along with olives. Not forgetting the pizza with speck and asparagus, once again playing on the balance of flavour dissonances.

Many of the ingredients I use are English. I continue to visit local farmers' markets, where I still meet up with the producers I bought from when first starting out and from whom I continue to source. The difference today is that they now ask to take a picture with me. I will never cease to be amazed!

primavera

A fresh delight with best quality prosciutto, cherry tomatoes and rocket/arugula.

Preheating the oven Preheat your oven to its highest temperature for at least 40 minutes.

Preparing the pizza base Begin with dough that has been allowed to rise properly. Roll out the dough ball on a lightly floured surface, forming a slightly raised edge around the sides (see page 15). Lift onto a baking sheet.

Adding the cheese Evenly spread the fior di latte over the pizza base and add a drizzle of extra virgin olive oil.

Initial baking Place the pizza at the bottom of the preheated oven (see page 10) and bake for about 5 minutes.

Final baking After 4–5 minutes, transfer the pizza to the upper part of the oven and switch to the grill/broil mode. Cook for about 2 minutes, or until the cheese has melted and the crust is lightly golden.

Finishing and serving Remove the pizza from the oven, add the rocket, proscuitto, semi-dried cherry tomatoes, some shavings of Parmigiano-Reggiano and a final drizzle of extra virgin olive oil. Let the pizza rest for a minute before slicing and serving.

1 ball Pizza Dough (see pages 12–15)
flour, for dusting
100 g/3½ oz. fior di latte,
    torn into pieces
extra virgin olive oil, to drizzle
30 g/1 oz. rocket/arugula
80 g/3 oz. prime quality proscuitto
40 g/1½ oz. semi-dried cherry
    tomatoes
Parmigiano-Reggiano shavings,
    to finish
a few fresh basil leaves

pesto e pomodorini

A flavourful pizza with fresh basil pesto and tomatoes.

Preheating the oven Preheat your oven to its highest temperature for at least 40 minutes.

Making the pesto Heat a small frying pan/skillet over a low heat. Add the pine nuts and cook until golden, shaking occasionally. Put the nuts into a food processor with the basil, Parmesan, olive oil and garlic clove. Whizz until smooth, then season to taste with salt and freshly ground black pepper.

Preparing the pizza base Begin with dough that has been allowed to rise properly. Roll out the dough ball on a lightly floured surface, forming a slightly raised edge around the sides (see page 15). Lift onto a baking sheet.

Adding the pesto Evenly spread all of the pesto over the pizza base, avoiding the edges.

Initial baking Place the pizza at the bottom of the preheated oven (see page 10) and bake for about 5 minutes.

Adding the cheeses After the initial 5 minutes of baking, when the base is nearly but not fully cooked, remove the pizza from the oven. Add the fior di latte and Provolone and sprinkle with grated Parmigiano-Reggiano.

Final baking Transfer the pizza to the upper part of the oven and switch to the grill/broil mode. Cook for about 2 minutes, or until the cheeses have melted and the crust is lightly golden.

Finishing and serving Remove the pizza from the oven and finish with the semi-dried cherry tomatoes, a sprinkle of toasted hazelnuts (if using) and a drizzle of extra virgin olive oil. Let the pizza rest for a minute before slicing and serving.

1 ball Pizza Dough (see pages 12–15)
flour, for dusting
80 g/½ cup Basil Pesto
  (see below)
100 g/3½ oz. fior di latte,
  torn into pieces
30 g/1 oz. Provolone, sliced
20 g/1 tablespoon grated
  Parmigiano-Reggiano
30 g/1 oz. semi-dried cherry
  tomatoes
a handful of toasted hazelnuts,
  crushed, to finish (optional)
extra virgin olive oil, to drizzle

FOR THE PESTO
50 g/⅓ cup pine nuts
80 g/3 oz. basil leaves
50 g/1¾ oz. grated Parmesan
150 ml/⅔ cup olive oil
1 garlic clove, peeled
salt and freshly ground black
  pepper

carcioffola

A truly seasonal delight with artichokes.

Preheating the oven Preheat your oven to its highest temperature for at least 40 minutes.

Preparing the artichoke cream Take half of the artichokes and make a cream by sautéing them in a pan with salt, pepper and oil for about 15 minutes until soft. Place in a blender and whizz to a purée, adding a little water to if necessary to achieve the desired consistency. Season to taste with salt and freshly ground black pepper. Set aside.

Preparing the pizza base Begin with dough that has been allowed to rise properly. Roll out the dough ball on a lightly floured surface, forming a slightly raised edge around the sides (see page 15). Lift onto a baking sheet.

Adding toppings Evenly spread the artichoke cream over the pizza base, avoiding the edges and add the remaining grilled artichokes and the black olives.

Initial baking Place the pizza at the bottom of the preheated oven (see page 10) and bake for about 5 minutes.

Adding the cheese After the initial 5 minutes of baking, when the base is nearly but not fully cooked, remove the pizza from the oven. Add the pieces of fior di latte.

Final baking Transfer the pizza to the upper part of the oven and switch to the grill/broil mode. Cook for about 2 minutes, or until the cheese has melted and the crust is lightly golden.

Finishing and serving Remove the pizza from the oven and finish with a sprinkle of chopped parsley, grated Pecorino Romano and a drizzle of extra virgin olive oil. Let the pizza rest for a minute before slicing and serving.

1 ball Pizza Dough (see pages 12–15)
flour, for dusting
150 g/5½ oz. chargrilled artichokes
30 g/1 oz. stoned/pitted black olives
80 g/2¾ oz. fior di latte, torn into pieces
extra virgin olive oil, to drizzle
freshly chopped flat-leaf parsley
20 g/3 tablespoons grated Pecorino Romano
salt and freshly ground black pepper

ragù bianco

A hearty pizza with a savoury white ragù and rich flavours.

Preheating the oven Preheat your oven to its highest temperature for at least 40 minutes.

Preparing the vegetables Cut the carrots, celery and onion into very small pieces. Put them in a pan with a little oil, salt and pepper. Cook for 10–15 minutes until tender, then transfer the mixture to a blender and blend to make it as smooth as possible.

Preparing the sausage Cook the fresh sausage in a separate pan, then cut it in pieces.

Preparing the pizza base Begin with dough that has been allowed to rise properly. Roll out the dough ball on a lightly floured surface, forming a slightly raised edge around the sides (see page 15). Lift onto a baking sheet.

Adding the toppings Evenly spread the vegetable mixture over the pizza base, avoiding the edges and add the cooked sausage.

Initial baking Place the pizza at the bottom of the preheated oven (see page 10) and bake for about 5 minutes.

Adding the cheese After the initial 5 minutes of baking, when the base is nearly but not fully cooked, remove the pizza from the oven and add the pieces of fior di latte.

Final baking Transfer the pizza to the upper part of the oven and switch to the grill/broil mode. Cook for about 2 minutes, or until the cheese has melted and the crust is lightly golden.

Finishing and serving Remove the pizza from the oven and finish with the grated Parmesan and a drizzle of olive oil. Let the pizza rest for a minute before slicing and serving.

1 ball Pizza Dough (see pages 12–15)
flour, for dusting
50 g/2 oz. carrots
50 g/2 oz. celery
20 g/¾ oz. onion
extra virgin olive oil, to drizzle
80 g/2¾ oz. fresh Italian sausage
80 g/2¾ oz. fior di latte,
   torn into pieces
20 g/1 tablespoon grated Parmesan
salt and freshly ground black
   pepper

pisello, prosciutto e parmigiano

Pea cream, cooked ham and Parmesan.

1 ball Pizza Dough (see pages 12–15)
flour, for dusting
100 g/⅔ cup frozen peas
extra virgin olive oil, to sauté and drizzle
80 g/2¾ oz. fior di latte, torn into pieces
80 g/2¾ oz. prime quality cooked ham
30 g/1 oz. Parmesan shavings
salt and freshly ground black pepper

Preheating the oven Preheat your oven to its highest temperature for at least 40 minutes.

Preparing the pea cream Put the peas in a frying pan/skillet with a splash of olive oil and a pinch of salt. Cook for 10–15 minutes until they break down to form a cream (add a splash of water if needed). Season with black pepper.

Preparing the pizza base Begin with dough that has been allowed to rise properly. Roll out the dough ball on a lightly floured surface, forming a slightly raised edge around the sides (see page 15). Lift onto a baking sheet.

Adding the pea cream Evenly spread the pea cream over the pizza base, avoiding the edges.

Initial baking Place the pizza at the bottom of the oven (see page 10) and bake for about 5 minutes.

Adding the cheese Remove the pizza from the oven and add the pieces of fior di latte.

Final baking Transfer the pizza to the upper part of the oven and switch to the grill/broil mode. Cook for about 2 minutes, or until the cheese has melted and the crust is lightly golden.

Finishing and serving Remove the pizza from the oven, and finish with the ham, Parmesan shavings and a drizzle of virgin olive oil. Let the pizza rest for a minute before slicing and serving.

burrata, basilico e acciughe

A rich blend of burrata, salty anchovies and crispy fried basil.

1 ball Pizza Dough (see pages 12–15)
flour, for dusting
a few fresh basil leaves
extra virgin olive oil, to drizzle
100 g/3½ oz. Basic Tomato Sauce (see page 18)
150 g/5½ oz. burrata, torn into pieces
6–7 canned anchovy fillets

Preheating the oven Preheat your oven to its highest temperature for at least 40 minutes.

Frying the basil Ensure the basil is not wet by patting the leaves with paper towels. Heat a splash of olive oil in a frying pan/skillet set over a high heat. Add the dry leaves and fry briefly until crisp. Set aside.

Preparing the pizza base Begin with dough that has been allowed to rise properly. Roll out the dough ball on a lightly floured surface, forming a slightly raised edge around the sides (see page 15). Lift onto a baking sheet.

Adding the tomato Evenly spread the tomato sauce over the pizza base, avoiding the edges.

Initial baking Place the pizza at the bottom of the oven (see page 10) and bake for about 5 minutes.

Final baking Transfer the pizza to the upper part of the oven and switch to the grill/broil mode. Cook for about 2 minutes, or until the crust is lightly golden.

Finishing and serving Remove the pizza from the oven and finish with the pieces of burrata, anchovy fillets and the fried basil leaves. Let the pizza rest for a minute before slicing and serving.

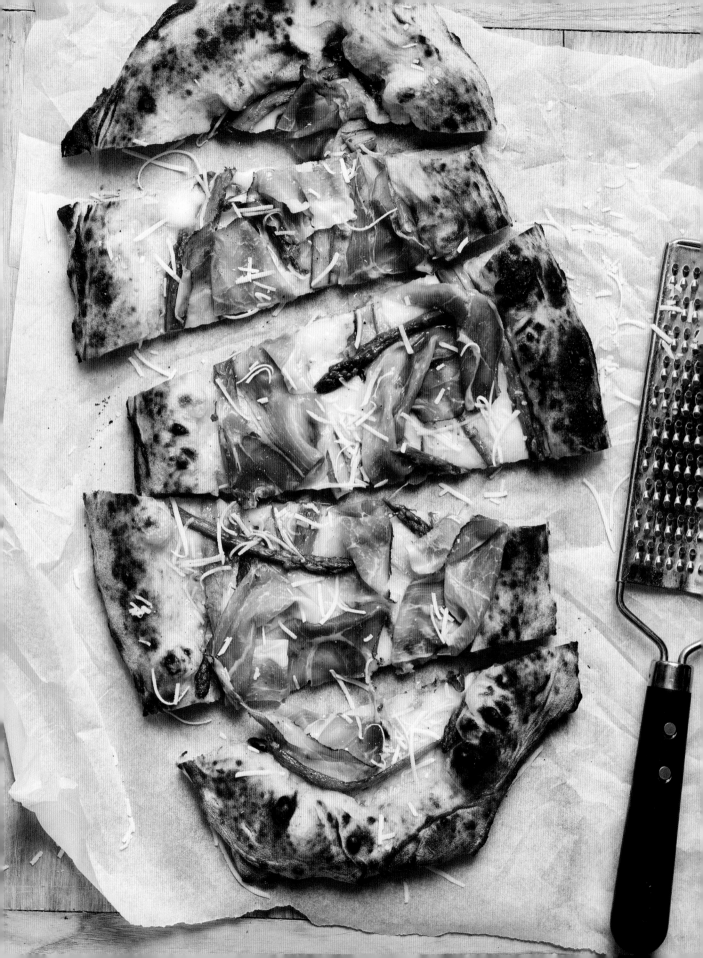

speck e asparago

A delightful pairing of speck (a cured, lightly smoked ham) and tender asparagus.

Preheating the oven Preheat your oven to its highest temperature for at least 40 minutes.

Preparing the asparagus Trim the asparagus, discarding any woody ends. Cut the spears lengthways to create thin, floppy slices. Heat a splash of olive oil in a frying pan/skillet and sauté the asparagus over a high heat. Season with salt and pepper. Set aside.

Preparing the pizza base Begin with dough that has been allowed to rise properly. Roll out the dough ball on a lightly floured surface, forming a slightly raised edge around the sides (see page 15). Lift onto a baking sheet.

Adding the cheese Evenly spread the fior di latte over the pizza base, avoiding the edges.

Initial baking Place the pizza at the bottom of the preheated oven (see page 10) and bake for about 5 minutes.

Final baking Transfer the pizza to the upper part of the oven and switch to the grill/broil mode. Cook for about 2 minutes, or until the cheese has melted and the crust is lightly golden.

Finishing and serving Remove the pizza from the oven and finish with the sautéed asparagus, speck, grated Pecorino Romano and a final drizzle of extra virgin olive oil. Let the pizza rest for a minute before slicing and serving.

1 ball Pizza Dough (see pages 12–15)
flour, for dusting
50 g/1¾ oz. young asparagus
extra virgin olive oil, to sauté and drizzle
100 g/3½ oz. fior di latte, torn into pieces
80 g/3 oz. speck
20 g/2 tablespoons grated Pecorino Romano
salt and freshly ground black pepper

margherita 2.0

A modern twist on the classic with tomato, creamy stracciatella and a vibrant basil pesto.

Preheating the oven Preheat your oven to its highest temperature for at least 40 minutes.

Preparing the pizza base Begin with dough that has been allowed to rise properly. Roll out the dough ball on a lightly floured surface, forming a slightly raised edge around the sides (see page 15). Lift onto a baking sheet.

Adding the topping Evenly spread the passata over the pizza base, avoiding the edges. Season with a pinch of salt.

Initial baking Place the pizza at the bottom of the preheated oven (see page 10) and bake for about 5 minutes.

Final baking Transfer the pizza to the upper part of the oven and switch to the grill/broil mode. Cook for about 2 minutes, or until the crust is lightly golden.

Finishing and serving Remove the pizza from the oven, and finish with the stracciatella, dots of basil pesto, fresh basil leaves and a drizzle of extra virgin olive oil. Let the pizza rest for a minute before slicing and serving.

1 ball Pizza Dough (see pages 12–15)
flour, for dusting
90 g/⅓ cup passata/strained
   tomatoes
70 g/2½ oz. fresh stracciatella
40 g/¼ cup Basil Pesto
   (see page 22)
a few fresh basil leaves
extra virgin olive oil, to drizzle
salt

pomodorini gialli, 'nduja e basilico

A unique creation with bold ingredients – yellow tomatoes, 'nduja (spreadable spicy Calabrian sausage) and fresh basil.

Preheating the oven Preheat your oven to its highest temperature for at least 40 minutes.

Preparing the cherry tomato cream Put the tomatoes in a pan and sauté over a low heat with a splash of olive oil. Season with salt and pepper and then blend to form a smooth purée. Set aside.

Preparing the pizza base Begin with dough that has been allowed to rise properly. Roll out the dough ball on a lightly floured surface, forming a slightly raised edge around the sides (see page 15). Lift onto a baking sheet.

Adding the toppings Spread the cherry tomato cream over the pizza base, avoiding the edges, and drizzle with a little oil.

Initial baking Place the pizza at the bottom of the preheated oven (see page 10) and bake for about 5 minutes.

Adding more toppings After the initial 5 minutes of baking, when the base is nearly but not fully cooked, remove the pizza from the oven. Add the 'nduja and pieces of fior di latte.

Final baking Transfer the pizza to the upper part of the oven and switch to the grill/broil mode. Cook for about 2 minutes, or until the cheese has melted and the crust is lightly golden.

Finishing and serving Remove the pizza from the oven and garnish with basil leaves and a final drizzle of extra virgin olive oil. Let the pizza rest for a minute before slicing and serving.

1 ball Pizza Dough (see pages 12–15)
flour, for dusting
100 g/3½ oz. yellow cherry tomatoes
extra virgin olive oil, to drizzle
40 g/1½ oz. 'nduja
80 g/2¾ oz. fior di latte, torn into pieces
a few fresh basil leaves
salt and freshly ground black pepper

Estate
SUMMER

celebrate the sunshine

The first thing that comes to mind when I think of summers past are the long July days spent with my grandmother making tomato preserves. Nowadays, you can easily buy them at the supermarket, but in Southern Italy where I come from, it's not uncommon for people to still make them in the traditional way.

In the days leading up, we would buy large quantities of tomatoes directly from farmers, hand-picking them and bringing them home. Then, around 3 am the real work began, involving the whole family and turning a necessary activity into a seasonal ritual that strengthened family bonds – a ritual I still miss and feel nostalgic for. We would clean the tomatoes, boil them, pass the juice through a food mill to remove the seeds, boil the empty glass bottles to sterilize them, bottle the juice and finally, boil the filled bottles, letting them cool for 24 hours. That tomato sauce would then be used throughout the year, capturing the extraordinary taste of fresh tomatoes without any preservatives.

I can't think of a better example to explain why seasonality in cooking is fundamental. The quality of the product, the cost, the environmental impact, the health benefits, the energy consumption – there are

many reasons why the scale tips in favour of seasonality. It's a rule the entire restaurant industry should adopt, even if it means accepting the idea of lower profits, but with greater respect for the planet, our customers and the deep mission of our work, which is to provide well-being through healthy nourishment. Today, we are used to finding any food at any time of the year, but my pizza remains a seasonal product. For this reason, our menu changes four times a year according to the seasons because each season has its own flavours, and our bodies have different needs at different times of the year.

My summer pizzas prioritize these needs. Summer is the season of tomatoes. I find the ones grown on the Isle of Wight excellent, and I regularly use them for my pizza. Among the many Italian varieties, there are some I consider indispensable. San Marzano, of course, and I must include the Pomodorino del Piennolo del Vesuvio DOP on my shortlist. These small tomatoes with thick skins are grown on the volcanic slopes of Vesuvius. The peculiar and fertile nature of the soil favours a high concentration of sugars, acids and minerals, making this tomato a product that naturally preserves for

a long time, also thanks to its cluster composition (literally a sort of pendulum), which is then hung in a dry and cool place. The flavour is particularly intense, sweet with a slightly acidic aftertaste, and varies over the months as the tomato matures and acquires new nuances. The Pomodorino del Piennolo is an almost universal ingredient in Neapolitan and Campanian cuisine, used in many typical dishes, and naturally, it cannot be missing from my pizza.

Another champion among tomatoes is the Corbarino. Small in size, with a shape reminiscent of a pear or a light bulb, it is grown in Campania, mainly on the hills of Corbara in the Agro Nocerino-Sarnese area, but also in the Pompeii and Castellammare di Stabia area, on the Amalfi coast, and in the Sorrento peninsula. A tomato with a sweet and sour flavour, traditionally produced in the hills without irrigation water, it owes its characteristics also to the thermal excursion, in areas of enormous historical significance and great tourist appeal.

But summer is not just all about tomatoes; it's also the season of aubergine (eggplant), courgettes (zucchini) and bell peppers, which therefore cannot be missing from my seasonal pizzas. The Parmigiana is regularly available from late May/early June until early September. Then we have the Nerano, inspired by the pasta dish typical of the Sorrento coast. A soft courgetti cream with Provolone del Monaco, crispy courgetti chips and smoked provola. In my Ortolana pizza, there are fresh cherry tomatoes, grilled courgettes, peppers and aubergines – a pizza you must eat in the summer to capture the nuances of the seasonal ingredients at their peak. To these vegetables, I then add cured meats in other pizzas, creating combinations that require a long process. It starts with the idea, imagining the pairings, testing months in advance, and only when the result convinces me and my staff does that pizza become part of the new menu. Seasonality, due to its importance, needs time. If you eat one of my pizzas in winter, you have to think that in my mind, it was conceived months before, and I offer it to you only when I know you won't be able to do without it. Until the season ends, of course...

ortolana

A garden-fresh mix of seasonal vegetables on a crispy crust.

Preheating the oven Preheat your oven to its highest temperature for at least 40 minutes.

Preparing the vegetables Slice the courgettes, aubergine and red peppers into 'julienne' strips (very fine). Heat a splash of olive oil in a frying pan/skillet and when sizzling, add the vegetables and cook briefly until tender. Remove from the pan and drain on paper towels. (If you prefer a lighter version, place the vegetable strips on a baking sheet and bake in the oven at the highest temperature for 20 minutes.)

Preparing the pizza base Begin with dough that has been allowed to rise properly. Roll out the dough ball on a lightly floured surface, forming a slightly raised edge around the sides (see page 15). Lift onto a baking sheet.

Adding the topping Spread the tomato sauce evenly over the pizza base, avoiding the edges. Season with a pinch of salt.

Initial baking Place the pizza at the bottom of the preheated oven (see page 10) and bake for about 5 minutes.

Adding the vegetables After the initial 5 minutes of baking, when the base is nearly but not fully cooked, remove the pizza from the oven. Add the sautéed vegetables and pieces of fior di latte.

Final baking Transfer the pizza to the upper part of the oven and switch to the grill/broil mode. Cook for about 2 minute, or until the cheese has melted and the crust is lightly golden.

Finishing and serving Remove the pizza from the oven, and finish with the semi-dried tomatoes, fresh basil leaves and a drizzle of extra virgin olive oil. Let the pizza rest for a minute before slicing and serving.

1 ball Pizza Dough (see pages 12–15)
flour, for dusting
50 g/2 oz. courgettes/zucchini
50 g/2 oz. aubergine/eggplant
50 g/2 oz. red (bell) pepper
**extra virgin olive oil, to sauté
    and drizzle**
**100 g/3½ oz. Basic Tomato Sauce
    (see page 18)**
**70 g/2½ oz. fior di latte,
    torn into pieces**
20 g/¾ oz. semi-dried tomatoes
a few fresh basil leaves
salt

nerano

A delicate balance of courgette (zucchini) and provolone.

Preparing the courgettes Cut half the courgettes into small pieces, place them in a pan with a little water, black pepper, salt and a splash of extra virgin olive oil. Simmer for 10 minutes over moderate heat until soft. Blend the mixture with a stick blender to make a cream. Cut the remaining courgettes into thin rounds using a mandoline or a sharp knife. Heat a little olive oil in a frying pan/skillet, add the courgettes and fry until they are crisp but not burnt.

Preheating the oven Preheat your oven to its highest temperature for at least 40 minutes.

Preparing the pizza base Begin with dough that has been allowed to rise properly. Roll out the dough ball on a lightly floured surface, forming a slightly raised edge around the sides (see page 15). Lift onto a baking sheet.

Adding ingredients Evenly spread the courgette cream over the pizza base and add a drizzle of extra virgin olive oil.

Initial baking Place the pizza at the bottom of the preheated oven (see page 10) and bake for about 5 minutes.

Adding the cheese After the initial 5 minutes of baking, when the base is nearly but not fully cooked, remove the pizza from the oven. Add the pieces of fior di latte.

Final baking Transfer the pizza to the upper part of the oven and switch to the grill/broil mode. Cook for about 2 minutes, or until the cheese has melted and the crust is lightly golden.

Finishing and serving Remove the pizza from the oven, add the fried courgette pieces, stracciatella and provolone and finish with a final drizzle of extra virgin olive oil. Let the pizza rest for a minute before slicing and serving.

1 ball Pizza Dough (see pages 12–15)
flour, for dusting
100 g/3½ oz. courgettes/zucchini
**extra virgin olive oil, to sauté
    and drizzle**
olive oil, for shallow frying
**80 g/3 oz. fior di latte,
    torn into pieces**
**100 g/3½ oz. stracciatella, pulled
    into pieces**
30 g/1 oz. provolone, shaved
**salt and freshly ground black
    pepper**

crudo e fichi

A sublime and elegant pairing of sweet, caramelized figs with salty Parma ham.

1 ball Pizza Dough (see pages 12–15)
flour, for dusting
50 g/2 oz. fresh figs, cut into thick wedges
2 teaspoons sugar
80 g/3 oz. fior di latte, torn into pieces
80 g/3 oz. Parma ham
a few fresh basil leaves
extra virgin olive oil, to drizzle

Preheating the oven Preheat your oven to its highest temperature for at least 40 minutes.

Preparing the figs Place the wedges of fig in a pan with the sugar. Cook for about 3–4 minutes, turn and cook for a further 3 minutes until caramelized and golden. Remove from the pan and set aside.

Preparing the pizza base Begin with dough that has been allowed to rise properly. Roll out the dough ball on a lightly floured surface, forming a slightly raised edge around the sides (see page 15). Lift onto a baking sheet.

Adding the topping Evenly spread the fior di latte over the pizza base, avoiding the edges.

Initial baking Place the pizza at the bottom of the preheated oven (see page 10) and bake for about 5 minutes.

Final baking Transfer the pizza to the upper part of the oven and switch to the grill/broil mode. Cook for about 2 minutes, or until the cheese has melted and the crust is lightly golden.

Finishing and serving Remove the pizza from the oven and finish with the caramelized figs and Parma ham. Add a final drizzle of extra virgin olive oil and a few basil leaves. Let the pizza rest for a minute before slicing and serving.

multicolore

A visual feast boasting a variety of vibrant cherry tomatoes.

1 ball Pizza Dough (see pages 12–15)
flour, for dusting
50 g/2 oz. yellow tomatoes, halved
50 g/2 oz. cherry tomatoes, halved
50 g/2 oz. semi-dried tomatoes
80 g/3 oz. fior di latte, torn into pieces
Parmigiano-Reggiano shavings, to finish
a few fresh basil leaves
extra virgin olive oil, to drizzle

Preheating the oven Preheat your oven to its highest temperature for at least 40 minutes.

Preparing the pizza base Begin with dough that has been allowed to rise properly. Roll out the dough ball on a lightly floured surface, forming a slightly raised edge around the sides (see page 15). Lift onto a baking sheet.

Adding the tomatoes Evenly spread the tomatoes over the pizza base, avoiding the edges, and add the pieces of fior di latte.

Initial baking Place the pizza at the bottom of the preheated oven (see page 10) and bake for about 5 minutes.

Final baking Transfer the pizza to the upper part of the oven and switch to the grill/broil mode. Cook it for about 2 minutes, or until the cheese has melted and the crust is lightly golden.

Finishing and serving Remove the pizza from the oven, finish with the Parmigiano-Reggiano shavings, basil leaves and a drizzle of extra virgin olive oil. Let the pizza rest for a minute before slicing and serving.

tonno e cipolle

A classic combination of tuna, sweet caramelized onions with crumbled oven-dried black olives (which need to be made in advance).

Preparing the olives in advance Turn the oven to its lowest setting. Place the olives in an ovenproof dish and bake for about 2–3 hours until they become very dry. Once they are completely dried and allowed to cool, they are ready to be turned into powder. You can crumble them to a dust with your fingers, or place them in a food processor or blender and whizz for a few seconds. Set aside.

Preheating the oven Preheat your oven to its highest temperature for at least 40 minutes.

Preparing the onion Cut the onion into very fine slices. Cook in a saucepan with a splash of olive oil over a very low heat for about 20 minutes. Then add a drop of balsamic vinegar and the sugar. Continue to cook, stirring occasionally, until soft and caramelized.

Preparing the pizza base Begin with dough that has been allowed to rise properly. Roll out the dough ball on a lightly floured surface, forming a slightly raised edge around the sides (see page 15). Lift onto a baking sheet.

Adding ingredients Evenly spread the salad leaves over the pizza base, avoiding the edges and add a drizzle of extra virgin olive oil. Place the pieces of fior di latte evenly on top to prevent the salad leaves from burning.

Initial baking Place the pizza at the bottom of the preheated oven (see page 10) and bake for about 5 minutes.

Adding the tomatoes After the initial 5 minutes of baking, when the base is nearly but not fully cooked, remove the pizza from the oven. Scatter over the semi-dried cherry tomatoes.

Final baking Transfer the pizza to the upper part of the oven and switch to the grill/broil mode. Cook for about 2 minutes, or until the cheese has melted and the crust is lightly golden.

Finishing and serving Remove the pizza from the oven and finish with the tuna, black olive powder and dots of caramelized onion. Let the pizza rest for a minute before slicing and serving.

1 ball Pizza Dough (see pages 12–15)
flour, for dusting
30 g/1 oz. stoned/pitted black olives
100 g/3½ oz. red onion
extra virgin olive oil, to sauté and drizzle
a dash of balsamic vinegar
4 teaspoons sugar
50 g/2 oz. curly escarole or lollo salad leaves
100 g/3½ oz. fior di latte, torn into pieces
30 g/1 oz. semi-dried cherry tomatoes
100 g/3½ oz. good-quality tuna fillets in olive oil (from a jar)

pancetta
e zucchini

A tasty combination of crispy smoked pancetta and tender summer courgettes (zucchini).

Preheating the oven Preheat your oven to its highest temperature for at least 40 minutes.

Preparing the courgettes Cut the courgettes into very thin slices lengthways. Heat a little olive oil in a frying pan/skillet and sauté the thin strips briefly over a high heat, seasoning them with salt and black pepper.

Preparing the pizza base Begin with dough that has been allowed to rise properly. Roll out the dough ball on a lightly floured surface, forming a slightly raised edge around the sides (see page 15). Lift onto a baking sheet.

Adding the toppings Evenly spread the pieces of fior di latte and the pancetta over the pizza base, avoiding the edges.

Initial baking Place the pizza at the bottom of the preheated oven (see page 10) and bake for about 5 minutes.

Adding the courgettes After the initial 5 minutes of baking, when the base is nearly but not fully cooked, remove the pizza from the oven. Spread the sautéed courgette strips evenly over the pizza.

Final baking Transfer the pizza to the upper part of the oven and switch to the grill/broil mode. Cook for about 2 minutes, or until the cheese has melted and the crust is lightly golden.

Finishing and serving Remove the pizza from the oven and sprinkle with shavings of Parmesan and a drizzle of extra virgin olive oil. Let the pizza rest for a minute before slicing and serving.

1 ball Pizza Dough (see pages 12–15)
flour, for dusting
100 g/3½ oz. courgettes/zucchini
olive oil, to sauté
80 g/3 oz. fior di latte,
    torn into pieces
80 g/3 oz. finely sliced smoked
    pancetta
20 g/¾ oz. Parmesan, shaved
salt and freshly ground black
    pepper
extra virgin olive oil, to drizzle

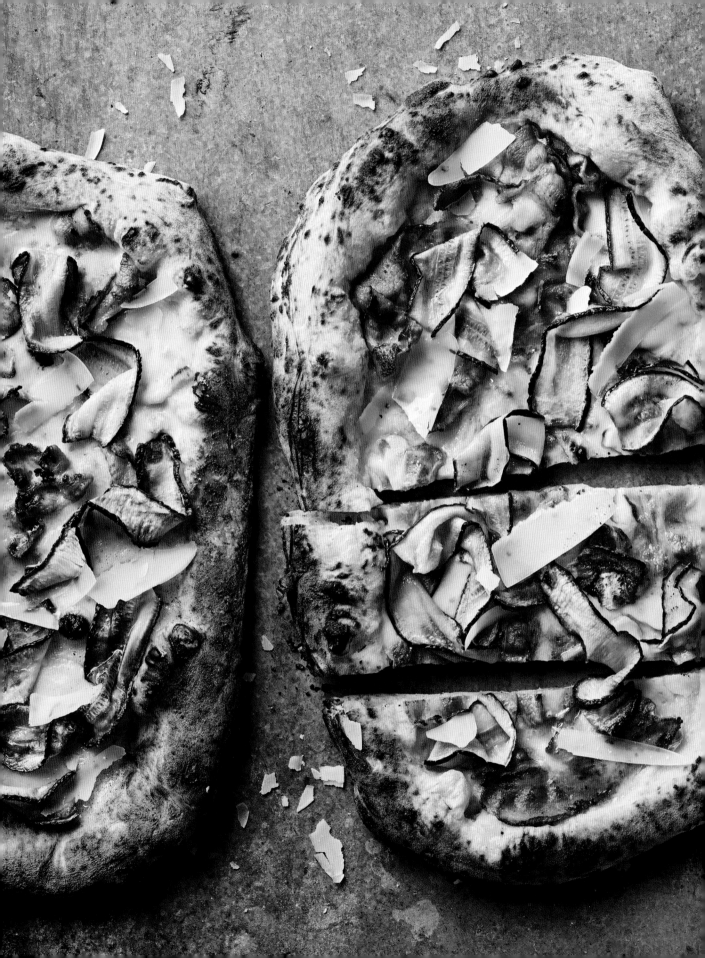

bresaola e arugula

A flavourful mix of bresaola (air-dried salted beef) and peppery rocket.

Preheating the oven Preheat your oven to its highest temperature for at least 40 minutes.

Preparing the pizza base Begin with dough that has been allowed to rise properly. Roll out the dough ball on a lightly floured surface, forming a slightly raised edge around the sides (see page 15). Lift onto a baking sheet.

Adding the toppings Evenly spread the tomato sauce and pieces of fior di latte over the pizza base, avoiding the edges.

Initial baking Place the pizza at the bottom of the preheated oven (see page 10) and bake for about 5 minutes.

Final baking Transfer the pizza to the upper part of the oven and switch to the grill/broil mode. Cook for about 2 minutes, or until the cheese has melted and the crust is lightly golden.

Finishing and serving Remove the pizza from the oven and finish with rocket, bresaola and a final drizzle of extra virgin olive oil. Add a light sprinkling of Parmigiano-Reggiano. Let the pizza rest for a minute before slicing and serving.

1 ball Pizza Dough (see pages 12–15)
flour, for dusting
50 g/3½ tablespoons Basic
    Tomato Sauce (see page 18)
80 g/3 oz. fior di latte,
    torn into pieces
30 g/1 oz. rocket/arugula
80 g/3 oz. bresaola
a pinch of finely grated
    Parmigiano-Reggiano, to finish
extra virgin olive oil, to drizzle

parmigiana

A blend of aubergine, tomato sauce and melted mozzarella.

Preparing the aubergines Slice the aubergine lengthways into
½-cm/¼-inch thick pieces, using either a mandoline or a sharp
knife. Heat the sunflower oil in a frying pan/skillet and immerse
the slices in the hot oil, frying them until they achieve a beautiful
golden hue. Drain on a plate lined with paper towels.

Preheating the oven Preheat your oven to its highest temperature
for at least 40 minutes.

Preparing the pizza base Begin with dough that has been allowed
to rise properly. Roll out the dough ball on a lightly floured surface,
forming a slightly raised edge around the sides (see page 15). Lift
onto a baking sheet.

Adding the tomato sauce Spread the tomato sauce evenly over
the pizza base, avoiding the edges.

Initial baking Place the pizza at the bottom of the preheated oven
(see page 10) and bake for about 5 minutes.

Adding the cheeses After the initial 5 minutes of baking, when
the base is nearly but not fully cooked, remove the pizza from the
oven. Add the pieces of fior di latte and slices of fried aubergine.

Final baking Transfer the pizza to the upper part of the oven and
switch to the grill/broil mode. Cook for about 2 minutes, or until
the cheese has melted and the crust is lightly golden.

Finishing and serving Remove the pizza from the oven, scatter
over the Parmigiano-Reggiano shavings and basil leaves and add a
drizzle of extra virgin olive oil. Let the pizza rest for a minute before
slicing and serving.

1 ball Pizza Dough (see pages 12–15)
flour, for dusting
1 aubergine/eggplant
   (about 100 g/3½ oz.)
100 ml/7 tablespoons sunflower oil
100 g/3½ oz. Basic Tomato Sauce
   (see page 18)
80 g/3 oz. fior di latte,
   torn into pieces
Parmigiano-Reggiano shavings,
   to finish
a few fresh basil leaves
extra virgin olive oil, to drizzle

'aubergine lovers'

A delightful treat for fans of this prized summer vegetable.

Preheating the oven Preheat your oven to its highest temperature for at least 40 minutes.

Frying the aubergines Slice half the aubergine lengthways into ½-cm/¼-inch thick pieces, using either a mandoline or a sharp knife. Heat the sunflower oil in a frying pan/skillet and immerse the slices in the hot oil, frying them until they achieve a beautiful golden hue. Remove the slices from the pan with a slotted spoon and drain on a plate lined with paper towels.

Making the aubergine cream Cut the remaining half an aubergine into small pieces and fry in the same pan (no need to wash it) for 5 minutes, or until soft. Drain on a plate lined with paper towels, then transfer to a blender and blend until you have a smooth, creamy mixture.

Preparing the pizza base Begin with dough that has been allowed to rise properly. Roll out the dough ball on a lightly floured surface, forming a slightly raised edge around the sides (see page 15). Lift onto a baking sheet.

Adding the topping Spread the aubergine cream evenly over the pizza base, avoiding the edges.

Initial baking Place the pizza at the bottom of the preheated oven (see page 10) and bake for about 5 minutes.

Adding the cheese After the initial 5 minutes of baking, when the base is nearly but not fully cooked, remove the pizza from the oven. Add the pieces of fior di latte.

Final baking Transfer the pizza to the upper part of the oven and switch to the grill/broil mode. Cook for about 2 minutes, or until the cheese has melted and the crust is lightly golden.

Finishing and serving Remove the pizza from the oven and finish with Parma ham slices and the fried aubergine slices. Scatter over a few basil leaves and add a drizzle of extra virgin olive oil. Let the pizza rest for a minute before slicing and serving.

1 ball Pizza Dough (see pages 12–15)
1 aubergine/eggplant
    (about 100 g/3½ oz.)
100 ml/7 tablespoons sunflower oil
flour, for dusting
80 g/3 oz. fior di latte,
    torn into pieces
80 g/3 oz. Parma ham
a few fresh basil leaves
extra virgin olive oil, to drizzle

Autunno

AUTUMN

a time to be bold

As summer fades Autumn (fall) arrives. The days are shorter, the nights grow longer. The clocks go back by an hour and the temperature starts to drop: to some people it may feel like the end of the world... Perhaps surprisingly we feel this way even in southern Italy, where I was born and raised, even though our summer is scorchingly hot and winter traditionally mild. For me the end of summer is as if the DJ has played the last track, the party is over and it is time to go home and wait it out for the next big event. However, every change of season also presents a new challenge, and the one created by the transition from summer to autumn is particularly welcome for me!

That is because I always find it enjoyable to rediscover flavours that have been tucked away out of sight and out of mind for months, but each time, I'm convinced there are still unexplored nuances that can be discovered only in the subtle play of pairings. Usually, these ideas come to me just as I'm going to bed after a day's work, but there is simply no escape – I have to get up and make notes.

Take the pumpkin, for example. The pumpkin is synonymous with autumn, a symbol of Halloween, the quintessential autumn festival. Many believe that the pumpkin is a vegetable, but it is actually a fruit with a texture that seems tailor-made for cooking, with an extraordinary and unconventional flavour. In Italy, we even make pasta with pumpkin, but we make pasta with everything, so pumpkin is a must on my autumn pizza menus.

Pumpkin is sweetish, so you always have to work on contrasts to harmonize with its flavour. For the pizza, I make a slightly spicy pumpkin cream that I pair with pancetta and Pecorino Romano, ingredients with a robust salinity. In this play of opposites, the individual flavours emerge, but also the synthesis of an overall taste that makes pumpkin pizza one of my most cherished creations.

However, autumn is the kingdom of friarielli, a presence so imposing that it invades winter with its bitter flavour. In English, friarielli are known as 'Neapolitan greens'. It's an extraordinarily accurate definition because friarielli are grown only in Naples and its surroundings – another testimony to the truly local origins of the so-called Italian cuisine I have already talked about. Friarielli are similar to broccoli, but they are not broccoli; they vaguely resemble kale but are not kale, nor Portuguese *grelos* or Chinese *kai-lan*. They are something else, typical and widely used in Naples, especially in combination with sausages, but also in many other dishes.

The origin of the name is uncertain. Some suggest it comes from the Spanish *frio-gelos*, winter broccoli. Others lean towards the derivation from the Neapolitan verb *frijere*, which means to fry in English. Even their use as a pizza ingredient is shrouded in legend. It is said that in February 1694 an anonymous Neapolitan woman, having accidentally run out of tomatoes, added them to the pizza she was preparing, frying them in lard. I can't tell you how true this legend is, but for centuries, the legendary flavour of friarielli has spread through the narrow streets of Naples and, clearly, also on my sausage and friarielli pizza called Santa Agnese. Agnese is my partner's mother, and every time we visit her in Italy, she prepares monumental portions of sausages and friarielli. It seemed only right to name the pizza after her.

Kale is another key ingredient in my autumn pizzas. Based on the preferences of Italians living in London, kale is one of the most appreciated English foods by my compatriots. I love it and use it for one of my pizzas along with hazelnuts, chilli and gorgonzola. Summer might be over, but we continue to celebrate at the table, don't we? And while celebrating, as the vibrant colours of summer give way to the darker tones of autumn, among our other pizzas is the spinach, Gorgonzola and pear pizza, best enjoyed with a glass of good red wine.

Autumn is also the time of year for fungi. There is a changing of the guard between the fresh Scorzone truffle, harvested from mid-May to the end of August, and the black truffle, from mid-November to mid-March. Italian truffles come in various varieties produced in different regions of the country. For my pizza, I pair it with potatoes, with their strong, earthy flavour and slightly bitter aftertaste, which I believe perfectly complements the wide variety of flavours, the rich texture, and the aromas of the potatoes. The truffle symbolizes the work I do when creating my autumn pizzas, gradually shifting from the light and bright shades of summer to the bolder, more intense flavours and autumnal colours.

zucca e pancetta

A cosy pizza with sweet pumpkin cream and salty pancetta.

Preheating the oven Preheat your oven to its highest temperature for at least 40 minutes.

Preparing the pumpkin cream Sauté the cubes of pumpkin in a pan with a splash of olive oil, a knob of butter, a little water and a pinch of salt and pepper until they become soft. Using a hand-held stick blender or food processor, blend the cooked pumpkin until you obtain a smooth cream. (Note: if you have pumpkin left you can thinly slice it using a Japanese mandoline and lightly char in a ridged grill pan – add these slices to the finished pizza, if liked.)

Preparing the pizza base Begin with dough that has been allowed to rise properly. Roll out the dough ball on a lightly floured surface, forming a slightly raised edge around the sides (see page 15). Lift onto a baking sheet

Adding the toppings Evenly spread the pumpkin cream over the pizza base, avoiding the edges, and add a drizzle of extra virgin olive oil.

Initial baking Place the pizza at the bottom of the preheated oven (see page 10) and bake for about 5 minutes.

Adding the cheeses After the initial 5 minutes of baking, when the base is nearly but not fully cooked, remove the pizza from the oven. Add the pieces of fior di latte and put the pancetta on top.

Final baking Transfer the pizza to the upper part of the oven and switch to the grill/broil mode. Cook for about 2 minutes, or until the cheese has melted and the crust is lightly golden.

Finishing and serving Remove the pizza from the oven, and finish with some shavings of Pecorino Romano and a final drizzle of extra virgin olive oil. Let the pizza rest for a minute before slicing and serving.

1 ball Pizza Dough (see pages 12–15)
flour, for dusting
150 g/5½ oz. fresh pumpkin, peeled and cut into small cubes (prepared weight)
extra virgin olive oil, to sauté and drizzle
a knob/pat of butter
80 g/3 oz. fior di latte, torn into pieces
80 g/3 oz. thinly sliced pancetta
a handful of Pecorino Romano shavings, to finish
salt and freshly ground black pepper

autunno

A seasonal special with warm, earthy flavours.

Preheating the oven Preheat your oven to its highest temperature for at least 40 minutes.

Preparing the butternut squash cream Add the cubes of butternut squash to a pan of boiling water and boil for 4–5 minutes, or until they soften. Drain, place the cubes in a blender and blend until smooth. Season with salt and pepper to taste.

Preparing the pizza base Begin with dough that has been allowed to rise properly. Roll out the dough ball on a lightly floured surface, forming a slightly raised edge around the sides (see page 15). Lift onto a baking sheet.

Adding the toppings Spread the butternut squash cream evenly over the pizza base, avoiding the edges.

Initial baking Place the pizza at the bottom of the preheated oven (see page 10) and bake for about 5 minutes.

Adding the mozzarella After the initial 5 minutes of baking, when the base is nearly but not fully cooked, remove the pizza from the oven and add the smoked mozzarella.

Final baking Transfer the pizza to the upper part of the oven and switch to the grill/broil mode. Cook for about 2 minutes, or until the cheese has melted and the crust is lightly golden.

Finishing and serving Remove the pizza from the oven, and finish with shaved provolone, fresh basil leaves and a drizzle of extra virgin olive oil. Let the pizza rest for a minute before slicing and serving.

1 ball Pizza Dough (see pages 12–15)
flour, for dusting
250 g/9 oz. butternut squash, peeled and cut into small cubes (prepared weight)
80 g/3 oz. smoked mozzarella, cut into matchsticks
60 g/2¼ oz. Provolone, shaved
a few fresh basil leaves
extra virgin olive oil, to drizzle
salt and freshly ground black pepper

salsiccia e broccole

A hearty pairing of pork sausage and tenderstem broccoli.

Preheating the oven Preheat your oven to its highest temperature for at least 40 minutes.

Preparing the pizza base Begin with dough that has been allowed to rise properly. Roll out the dough ball on a lightly floured surface, forming a slightly raised edge around the sides (see page 15). Lift onto a baking sheet

Cooking the sausage Cut the sausage into small pieces, place in a small frying pan/skillet and sauté without oil until well cooked.

Cooking the broccoli In another pan, very gently sauté the tenderstem broccoli in a splash of olive oil with a pinch of salt and some black pepper.

Adding the toppings Evenly scatter the pieces of fior di latte and the cooked sausage pieces over the pizza base, then add a drizzle of extra virgin olive oil.

Initial baking Place the pizza at the bottom of the preheated oven (see page 10) and bake for about 5 minutes.

Adding the broccoli After the initial 5 minutes of baking, when the base is nearly but not fully cooked, remove the pizza from the oven. Add the sautéed broccoli.

Final baking Transfer the pizza to the upper part of the oven and switch to the grill/broil mode. Cook for about 2 minutes, or until the cheese has melted and the crust is lightly golden.

Finishing and serving Remove the pizza from the oven and finish with the Pecorino Romano, a grinding of black pepper and a final drizzle of extra virgin olive oil. Let the pizza rest for a minute before slicing and serving.

1 ball Pizza Dough (see pages 12–15)
flour, for dusting
100 g/3½ oz. fresh pork sausage
75 g/3 oz. tenderstem broccoli/
  broccolini
extra virgin olive oil, to sauté
  and drizzle
100 g/3½ oz. fior di latte,
  torn into pieces
30 g/1 oz. Pecorino Romano, grated
salt and freshly ground black
  pepper

cavolo, nocciole e peperoncino

A bold mix of kale, crunchy hazelnuts and a just a hint of chilli heat.

1 ball Pizza Dough (see pages 12–15)
flour, for dusting
120 g/4½ oz. cavolo nero (black kale) or kale
extra virgin olive oil, to drizzle
80 g/3 oz. fior di latte, torn into pieces
30 g/1 oz. toasted hazelnuts, crushed
1 teaspoon dried chilli/hot red pepper flakes
salt and freshly ground black pepper

Preheating the oven Preheat your oven to its highest temperature for at least 40 minutes.

Preparing the cavolo nero Chop into bite-sized pieces and discard any tough stems. Place in a pan of boiling water and boil for about 10 minutes or until it softens. Drain and season with salt, pepper and oil.

Preparing the pizza base Begin with dough that has been allowed to rise properly. Roll out the dough ball on a lightly floured surface, forming a slightly raised edge around the sides (see page 15). Lift onto a baking sheet

Adding the cheese Evenly spread the pieces of fior di latte over the pizza base, avoiding the edges.

Initial baking Place the pizza at the bottom of the oven (see page 10) and bake for about 5 minutes.

Final baking Transfer the pizza to the upper part of the oven and switch to the grill/broil mode. Cook for about 2 minutes, or until the cheese has melted and the crust is lightly golden.

Finishing and serving Remove the pizza from the oven, and finish with cavolo nero, crushed hazelnuts, chilli flakes and a drizzle of extra virgin olive oil. Let the pizza rest for a minute before slicing and serving.

gorgonzola e pera

A sweet and tangy pairing of Gorgonzola cheese and juicy pears.

1 ball Pizza Dough (see pages 12–15)
flour, for dusting
80 g/3 oz. fior di latte, torn into pieces
50 g/2 oz. Gorgonzola, cut into pieces
1 pear, cored and thinly sliced
2 teaspoons runny honey

Preheating the oven Preheat your oven to its highest temperature for at least 40 minutes.

Preparing the pizza base Begin with dough that has been allowed to rise properly. Roll out the dough ball on a lightly floured surface, forming a slightly raised edge around the sides (see page 15). Lift onto a baking sheet.

Adding the cheeses Evenly spread the pieces of fior di latte and Gorgonzola over the pizza base, avoiding the edges.

Initial baking Place the pizza at the bottom of the oven (see page 10) and bake for about 5 minutes.

Final baking Transfer the pizza to the upper part of the oven and switch to the grill/broil mode. Cook for about 2 minutes, or until the cheese has melted and the crust is lightly golden.

Finishing and serving Remove the pizza from the oven and finish with pear slices and drizzle over the honey. Let the pizza rest for a minute before slicing and serving.

Saint Agnese

A Neapolitan classic with pork sausage and bitter friarielli (see page 111).

Preheating the oven Preheat your oven to its highest temperature for at least 40 minutes.

Preparing the friarielli Place the greens in a frying pan/skillet with a splash of olive oil, a little salt, the chilli and garlic. Sauté until the greens are soft and well cooked. Transfer half the greens to a bowl and mix with a mini stick blender to make a purée; set the remaining half aside. Reserve the rest.

Cooking the sausage Cook the sausage slowly in the pan, then cut it into small pieces.

Preparing the pizza base Begin with dough that has been allowed to rise properly. Roll out the dough ball on a lightly floured surface, forming a slightly raised edge around the sides (see page 15). Lift onto a baking sheet

Adding the toppings Spread the blended friarielli evenly over the pizza base, avoiding the edges, then add the reserved sautéed friarielli and the sausage pieces.

Initial baking Place the pizza at the bottom of the preheated oven (see page 10) and bake for about 5 minutes.

Adding the cheese After the initial 5 minutes of baking, when the base is nearly but not fully cooked, remove the pizza from the oven. Add the smoked mozzarella.

Final baking Transfer the pizza to the upper part of the oven and switch to the grill/broil mode. Cook for about 2 minutes, or until the cheese has melted and the crust is lightly golden.

Finishing and serving Remove the pizza from the oven, finish with the Parmigiano-Reggiano and a drizzle of extra virgin olive oil. Let the pizza rest for a minute before slicing and serving.

1 ball Pizza Dough (see pages 12–15)
flour, for dusting
100 g/3½ oz. friarielli (Neapolitan greens)
extra virgin olive oil, to sauté and drizzle
1 fresh red chilli/chile, crushed, or a pinch of dried chilli/hot red pepper flakes
2 garlic cloves, crushed
70 g/2½ oz. fresh pork sausage
100 g/3½ oz. smoked mozzarella, cut into matchsticks
1½ tablespoons grated Parmigiano-Reggiano
salt and freshly ground black pepper

tartufo e patate

A luxurious blend of truffle and roasted potatoes.

Preheating the oven Preheat your oven to its highest temperature for at least 40 minutes.

Preparing the mozzarella Cut the smoked mozzarella into narrow strips, place in a sieve/strainer and let it drain for about 30 minutes to prevent it from releasing too much water during cooking.

Preparing the potatoes Peel the potatoes and cut them into small cubes. Place in a pan of boiling water and boil for a couple of minutes. Drain the potatoes, then sauté them in a pan with a little truffle oil, salt and pepper until they become slightly golden and crispy.

Preparing the pizza base Begin with dough that has been allowed to rise properly. Roll out the dough ball on a lightly floured surface, forming a slightly raised edge around the sides (see page 15). Lift onto a baking sheet

Adding the toppings Spread the sautéed potato cubes and smoked mozzarella evenly over the pizza base, avoiding the edges.

Initial baking Place the pizza at the bottom of the preheated oven (see page 10) and bake for about 5 minutes.

Final baking Transfer the pizza to the upper part of the oven and switch to the grill/broil mode. Cook for about 2 minutes, or until the cheese has melted and the crust is lightly golden.

Finishing and serving Remove the pizza from the oven and finish with freshly shaved black truffle and a drizzle of truffle oil. Let the pizza rest for a minute before slicing and serving.

1 ball Pizza Dough (see pages 12–15)
flour, for dusting
80 g/3 oz. smoked mozzarella
100 g/3½ oz. potatoes
   (approx. 2 medium potatoes)
1 teaspoon truffle oil,
   plus extra for drizzling
15 g/½ oz. fresh black truffle
salt and freshly ground black
   pepper

pizza spinaci e capocollo

A mix of fresh spinach and rich capocollo.

1 ball Pizza Dough (see pages 12–15)
flour, for dusting
150 g/5½ oz. fresh spinach leaves
extra virgin olive oil, to sauté and drizzle
a knob/pat of butter
80 g/3 oz. fior di latte, torn into pieces
80 g/3 oz. thinly sliced capocollo (or Parma ham)
salt and freshly ground black pepper

Preheating the oven Preheat your oven to its highest temperature for at least 40 minutes.

Preparing the spinach cream Place the spinach in a pan with a splash of olive oil, the butter and a pinch each of salt and pepper. Sauté until soft, then blend to make a spinach cream.

Preparing the pizza base Begin with dough that has been allowed to rise properly. Roll out the dough ball on a lightly floured surface, forming a slightly raised edge around the sides (see page 15). Lift onto a baking sheet

Adding the toppings Spread the spinach cream evenly over the pizza base, avoiding the edges, and add a drizzle of extra virgin olive oil.

Initial baking Place the pizza at the bottom of the oven (see page 10) and bake for about 5 minutes.

Adding the cheeses Remove the pizza from the oven and add the pieces of fior di latte.

Final baking Transfer the pizza to the upper part of the oven and switch to the grill/broil mode. Cook for about 2 minutes, or until the cheese has melted and the crust is lightly golden.

Finishing and serving Remove the pizza from the oven and finish with the capocollo and a drizzle of extra virgin olive oil. Let the pizza rest for a minute before slicing and serving.

mortazza

A truly gourmet combination of creamy mortadella and crunchy pistachios.

1 ball Pizza Dough (see pages 12–15)
flour, for dusting
50 g/2 oz. ricotta
80 g/3 oz. fior di latte, torn into pieces
100 g/3½ oz. mortadella (4 slices)
30 g/2 tablespoons Pistachio Pesto (see page 22)
20 g/¾ oz. crushed pistachios
salt

Preheating the oven Preheat your oven to its highest temperature for at least 40 minutes.

Preparing the ricotta In a small bowl, mix the ricotta with a bit of salt and water to create a smooth cream. Set aside.

Preparing the pizza base Begin with dough that has been allowed to rise properly. Roll out the dough ball on a lightly floured surface, forming a slightly raised edge around the sides (see page 15). Lift onto a baking sheet

Adding the toppings Spread the ricotta cream and fior di latte pieces evenly over the pizza base, avoiding the edges.

Initial baking Place the pizza at the bottom of the oven (see page 10) and bake for about 5 minutes.

Final baking Transfer the pizza to the upper part of the oven and switch to the grill/broil mode. Cook for about 2 minutes, or until the cheese has melted and the crust is lightly golden.

Finishing and serving Remove the pizza from the oven and finish with the mortadella slices, Pistachio Pesto and crushed pistachios. Let the pizza rest for a minute before slicing and serving.

Inverno
WINTER

a season of nostalgia

Winter, for me, is my grandmother's Sunday morning ragù. I started working in the restaurant industry early and would come home very late on Saturday nights. I would wake up on Sunday morning to the smell of ragù, so intense that I can still sense it in my nose as if it were yesterday. It's one of those memories that makes me wish for a time machine to go back to those winter mornings, with the windows fogged up by steam, keeping the December, January and February cold outside. Huge tables, with many people participating in one of the most heartfelt collective rituals of Neapolitan and Italian identity, where the conviviality of food is a central element of our culture.

Once out of bed, a positional war with my grandmother would begin with my cousins, waiting for her to get distracted or busy with something else. Once that happened, we would quietly approach the gigantic pot where the ragù had been simmering for hours at an incredibly slow pace, so slow that it would generate one isolated bubble at a time. When the manoeuvre was successful, we would dip the fresh bread bought that morning into the sauce, sprinkle it with Parmesan and continue until our grandmother noticed and chased us out of the kitchen. This was an

appetizer while waiting for the anticipated pasta dressed with ragù, the beef and pork meat, sausages and meatballs that we would eat during the endless lunch that included many (many) other courses.

It's no coincidence that my pizza Ricordi d'Infanzia has been on the menu since day one and is regularly one of the best sellers. The topping is made of a cream of Neapolitan ragù, pieces of meat, 24-month aged Parmigiano-Reggiano, basil and extra virgin olive oil. It is the pizza that more than any other tells my story, my roots and the culinary tradition of the place I come from. Ragù is also made in northern Italy, but it's known there as Bolognese and is made with minced meat, equally good and more famous internationally. In Naples, however, large, square pieces of meat are used, which the long, slow cooking renders extremely tender. My grandmother made it this way, having learned from her grandmother, thus continuing to thread the tradition through generations. That's the ragù you'll find on my pizza.

In winter, it's cold and we need calories to stay warm and stronger flavours to bring to the table. Therefore, my winter pizzas still feature friarielli (Neapolitan greens) with sausages, but also porcini

mushrooms that edge into winter, truffles and other seasonal products.

One pizza I am particularly proud of, with its strong flavours, is the Cheesewick. It's a play on words as Chiswick is the London neighbourhood that is home to my first pizzeria. There's a lot of study, work and testing behind a pizza that combines typical Campanian dairy products like ricotta and buffalo stracciatella, Blue Stilton, piennolo tomatoes and a cherry tomato cream. When a pizza manages to find the right balance between contrasting flavours and ingredients from different places, instead of stopping to admire the result, I tell myself that it can be done. This is what drives me to continually seek the next step, the next move forward to find other combinations, with a notebook and pen always ready on the bedside table to capture late-night ideas.

One of these is, for example, the Cacio e Pepe, a pizza derived from the typical Roman dish with pasta and cheese, reimagined. Pecorino is a hard cheese made from sheep's milk typical of the Mediterranean area. In Italy, it is produced in many regions but only from Emilia Romagna southwards, with different nuances and eight varieties recognized as DOP. It's a southern cheese, whose aromatic, slightly spicy and strong flavour tells stories of shepherds and livestock migration. It holds a place of honour on my Cacio e Pepe, also enriched with a selection of four different types of pepper.

Christmas is of course celebrated at the beginning of winter, but after Christmas, my mind is already fast-forwarding towards the rebirth of spring, even though the winter months are still ahead of me. Good nutrition is important in the season of colds and other illnesses. I always keep this in mind when developing my menus by choosing seasonal ingredients as much as possible, long-aged cheeses like provolone and smoked provola, but also dairy products like buffalo mozzarella, ricotta, Parmigiano-Reggiano and fior di latte, pairing them with greens such as broccoli, spinach, cabbage and friarielli. A triumph for the taste buds and a source of nourishment in the harshest season of the year.

ricordi d'infanzia

A nostalgic delight with rich ragù, evoking precious childhood memories (see page 132).

Preheating the oven Preheat your oven to its highest temperature for at least 40 minutes.

Preparing the pizza base Begin with dough that has been allowed to rise properly. Roll out the dough ball on a lightly floured surface, forming a slightly raised edge around the sides (see page 15). Lift onto a baking sheet.

Adding the sauces Spread the tomato sauce and the ragù evenly over the pizza base, avoiding the edges. Season with a pinch of salt.

Initial baking Place the pizza at the bottom of the preheated oven (see page 10) and bake for about 5 minutes.

Final baking Transfer the pizza to the upper part of the oven and switch to the grill/broil mode. Cook for about 2 minutes, or until the cheese has melted and the crust is lightly golden.

Finishing and serving Remove the pizza from the oven and finish with grated Parmigiano-Reggiano, Parmigiano-Reggiano cream, a few fresh basil leaves and a drizzle of extra virgin olive oil. Let the pizza rest for a minute before slicing and serving.

1 ball Pizza Dough (see pages 12–15)
flour, for dusting
30 g/2 tablespoons Basic Tomato Sauce (see page 18)
100 g/3½ oz. Neapolitan Ragù (see page 21)
30 g/1 oz. Parmigiano-Reggiano, grated
4–5 tablespoons Parmigiano-Reggiano Cream (see page 26)
a few fresh basil leaves
extra virgin olive oil, to drizzle
salt

'cheesewick'

A now famous blend of assorted cheeses, crafted by me, Michele Pascarella at Napoli on the Road in Chiswick.

Making the Parmigiano-Reggiano chips Place the finely grated Parmigiano-Reggiano on a small sheet of baking paper to form a layer about 5 mm/¼ inches thick. Cook in the microwave for about 1½ minutes, take it out slowly from the paper and set aside for 1–2 minutes or until dry.

Preheating the oven Preheat your oven to its highest temperature for at least 40 minutes.

Preparing the pizza base Begin with dough that has been allowed to rise properly. Roll out the dough ball on a lightly floured surface, forming a slightly raised edge around the sides (see page 15). Lift onto a baking sheet.

Adding two cheeses Spread the ricotta cheese evenly over the pizza base, avoiding the edges, then add the buffalo mozzarella.

Initial baking Place the pizza at the bottom of the preheated oven (see page 10) and bake for about 5 minutes.

Final baking Transfer the pizza to the upper part of the oven and switch to the grill/broil mode. Cook for about 2 minutes, or until the cheese has melted and the crust is lightly golden.

Finishing and serving Remove the pizza from the oven, add the Parmigiano-Reggiano chips, the pieces of Stilton and the stracciatella. Dot the pizza with about 14 small blobs of Creamy Piennolo Cherry Tomato Jam and finish with a drizzle of extra virgin olive oil. Let the pizza rest for a minute before slicing and serving.

1 ball Pizza Dough (see pages 12–15)
flour, for dusting
100 g/3½ oz. Parmigiano-Reggiano, finely grated
30 g/1 oz. ricotta cheese
80 g/3 oz. buffalo mozzarella, torn into pieces
30 g/1 oz. dry blue Stilton, broken into small pieces
40 g/1½ oz. stracciatella
about 60 ml/¼ cup Creamy Piennolo Cherry Tomato Jam (see page 18)
extra virgin olive oil, to drizzle

porcini, arugula e parmigiano

An earthy mix of porcini mushrooms, hot and peppery rocket and Parmesan.

Preheating the oven Preheat your oven to its highest temperature for at least 40 minutes.

Preparing the mushrooms Cut the mushrooms into pieces. Heat a little extra virgin olive oil in a pan, add the mushrooms and sauté, seasoning them with salt and pepper.

Preparing the pizza base Begin with dough that has been allowed to rise properly. Roll out the dough ball on a lightly floured surface, forming a slightly raised edge around the sides (see page 15). Lift onto a baking sheet.

Adding the toppings Spread the fior di latte and sautéed porcini mushrooms evenly over the pizza base, avoiding the edges.

Initial baking Place the pizza at the bottom of the preheated oven (see page 10) and bake for about 5 minutes.

Final baking Transfer the pizza to the upper part of the oven and switch to the grill/broil mode. Cook for about 2 minutes, or until the cheese has melted and the crust is lightly golden.

Finishing and serving Remove the pizza from the oven and finish with the rocket, grated Parmesan and a drizzle of extra virgin olive oil. Let the pizza rest for a minute before slicing and serving.

1 ball Pizza Dough (see pages 12–15)
flour, for dusting
80 g/3 oz. fresh porcini mushrooms
extra virgin olive oil, to sauté
 and drizzle
80 g/3 oz. fior di latte,
 torn into pieces
30 g/1 oz. rocket/arugula
30 g/1 oz. Parmesan, grated
salt and freshly ground black
 pepper

salsiccia e porcini

A satisfying combination of sausages with umami-rich porcini mushrooms and smoked mozzarella.

Preheating the oven Preheat your oven to its highest temperature for at least 40 minutes.

Cooking the sausage Break the sausage into small pieces, place in a small frying pan/skillet with a splash of extra virgin olive oil and cook gently for 15–20 minutes, stirring occasionally.

Preparing the pizza base Begin with dough that has been allowed to rise properly. Roll out the dough ball on a lightly floured surface, forming a slightly raised edge around the sides (see page 15). Lift onto a baking sheet.

Adding the toppings Spread the sliced porcini mushrooms, cooked sausage pieces and smoked mozzarella evenly over the pizza base.

Initial baking Place the pizza at the bottom of the preheated oven (see page 10) and bake for about 5 minutes.

Final baking Transfer the pizza to the upper part of the oven and switch to the grill/broil mode. Cook for about 2 minutes, or until the cheese has melted and the crust is lightly golden.

Finishing and serving Remove the pizza from the oven, finish with shavings of Parmigiano-Reggiano and a drizzle of extra virgin olive oil. Let the pizza rest for a minute before slicing and serving.

1 ball Pizza Dough (see pages 12–15)
flour, for dusting
100 g/3 oz. fresh pork sausage
extra virgin olive oil, to sauté and drizzle
80 g/2¾ oz. fresh porcini mushrooms, finely sliced
80 g/2¾ oz. smoked mozzarella, cut into matchsticks or small cubes
30 g/1 oz. Parmigiano-Reggiano, shaved

'curly'

A playful twist with a fresh tomato sauce and Italian sausage.

Preheating the oven Preheat your oven to its highest temperature for at least 40 minutes.

Cooking the sausage Break the sausage into small pieces, place in a small frying pan/skillet with a splash of extra virgin olive oil and cook gently for 15–20 minutes, stirring occasionally.

Preparing the pizza base Begin with dough that has been allowed to rise properly. Roll out the dough ball on a lightly floured surface, forming a slightly raised edge around the sides (see page 15). Lift onto a baking sheet.

Adding toppings Spread the tomato sauce and cooked sausage pieces evenly over the pizza base, avoiding the edges. Season with a pinch of salt.

Initial baking Place the pizza at the bottom of the preheated oven (see page 10) and bake for about 5 minutes.

Adding the cheese After the initial 5 minutes of baking, when the base is nearly but not fully cooked, remove the pizza from the oven and add the pieces of fior di latte.

Final baking Transfer the pizza to the upper part of the oven and switch to the grill/broil mode. Cook for about 2 minutes, or until the cheese has melted and the crust is lightly golden.

Finishing and serving Remove the pizza from the oven and finish with fresh basil leaves and a drizzle of extra virgin olive oil. Let the pizza rest for a minute before slicing and serving.

1 ball Pizza Dough (see pages 12–15)
flour, for dusting
80 g/3 oz. fresh Italian sausage
extra virgin olive oil, to sauté and drizzle
120 g/4½ oz. Basic Tomato Sauce (see page 18)
80 g/3 oz. fior di latte, torn into pieces
a few fresh basil leaves
salt

fungi e tartufo

An indulgent pairing of earthy mushrooms, smoked mozzarella and fragrant truffle oil.

Preheating the oven Preheat your oven to its highest temperature for at least 40 minutes.

Making the truffle cream Heat the olive oil in a pan over a medium heat. Add the garlic and shallot and sauté for about 2 minutes until fragrant. Add the sliced mushrooms and cook for about 10 minutes until tender and any liquid released has evaporated. Transfer the mixture to a food processor. Add the cream, grated Parmesan and truffle oil. Blend until smooth and creamy. If the mixture is too thick, add a little more cream or olive oil to reach your desired consistency. Season with salt and pepper, then blend again briefly to incorporate the seasoning. Set aside.

Preparing the shiitake mushrooms Sauté the shiitake mushrooms in a pan with a little olive oil and season with salt and pepper.

Preparing the pizza base Begin with dough that has been allowed to rise properly. Roll out the dough ball on a lightly floured surface, forming a slightly raised edge around the sides (see page 15). Lift onto a baking sheet.

Adding the toppings Spread the truffle cream and sautéed mushrooms evenly over the pizza base, avoiding the edges.

Initial baking Place the pizza at the bottom of the preheated oven (see page 10) and bake for about 5 minutes.

Adding the cheese After the initial 5 minutes of baking, when the base is nearly but not fully cooked, remove the pizza from the oven. Add the pieces of smoked mozzarella.

Final baking Transfer the pizza to the upper part of the oven and switch to the grill/broil mode. Cook for about 2 minutes, or until the cheese has melted and the crust is lightly golden.

Finishing and serving Remove the pizza from the oven, and finish with chopped parsley and a drizzle of truffle oil. Let the pizza rest for a minute before slicing and serving.

1 ball Pizza Dough (see pages 12–15)
flour, for dusting
80 g/3 oz. fresh shiitake or chestnut mushrooms, sliced
extra virgin olive oil, to sauté
80 g/3 oz. smoked mozzarella, cut into matchsticks
freshly chopped flat-leaf parsley
truffle oil, to drizzle

TRUFFLE CREAM
2 tablespoons olive oil
1 garlic clove, finely chopped
1 shallot, finely chopped
200 g/7 oz. fresh mushrooms (such as porcini or cremini), sliced
100 ml/⅓ cup plus 1 tablespoon double/heavy cream
50 g/2 oz. Parmesan, grated
2 tablespoons truffle oil
salt and freshly ground black pepper

broccolo

A wholesome and nourishing pizza topped with tenderstem broccoli.

1 ball Pizza Dough (see pages 12–15)
flour, for dusting
1 medium potato, peeled and cut into cubes
extra virgin olive oil, to sauté and drizzle
80 g/3 oz. tenderstem broccoli/broccolini
80 g/3 oz. smoked mozzarella, cut into matchsticks
dried chilli/hot red pepper flakes, to sprinkle
salt and freshly ground black pepper

Preheating the oven Preheat your oven to its highest temperature for at least 40 minutes.

Preparing the potato Cook the cubed potato in boiling water for about 2 minutes, until tender. Drain, then sauté in a frying pan/skillet with a splash of olive oil and a pinch of salt.

Preparing the broccoli Sauté the broccoli in a frying pan/skillet over a low heat with a splash of extra virgin olive oil. Cook for 10–15 minutes until crispy. Season with salt and pepper.

Initial baking Place the pizza at the bottom of the oven (see page 10) and bake for about 5 minutes.

Adding the toppings Spread the pieces of smoked mozzarella, potatoes and sautéed broccoli evenly over the pizza base, avoiding the edges.

Final baking Transfer the pizza to the upper part of the oven and switch to the grill/broil mode. Cook for about 2 minutes, or until the cheese has melted and the crust is lightly golden.

Finishing and serving Remove the pizza from the oven and add a sprinkle of chilli flakes and a drizzle of extra virgin olive oil. Let the pizza rest for a minute before slicing and serving.

pecorino e guanciale

A rich combination of Pecorino Romano cheese and crispy guanciale.

1 ball Pizza Dough (see pages 12–15)
flour, for dusting
120 g/4½ oz. Basic Tomato Sauce (see page 18)
100 g/3½ oz. finely sliced guanciale
40 g/scant ⅔ cup finely grated Pecorino Romano
extra virgin olive oil, to drizzle

Preheating the oven Preheat your oven to its highest temperature for at least 40 minutes.

Preparing the pizza base Begin with dough that has been allowed to rise properly. Roll out the dough ball on a lightly floured surface, forming a slightly raised edge around the sides (see page 15). Lift onto a baking sheet.

Adding the toppings Spread the tomato sauce and sliced guanciale evenly over the pizza base, avoiding the edges.

Initial baking Place the pizza at the bottom of the oven (see page 10) and bake for about 5 minutes.

Final baking Transfer the pizza to the upper part of the oven and switch to the grill/broil mode. Cook for about 2 minutes, or until the crust is lightly golden.

Finishing and serving Remove the pizza from the oven, and finish with grated Pecorino Romano and a drizzle of extra virgin olive oil. Let the pizza rest for a minute before slicing and serving.

salmone, erbe cipollina e ricotta

A delicate yet luxurious combination of smoked salmon, fresh chives and creamy ricotta.

Preheating the oven Preheat your oven to its highest temperature for at least 40 minutes.

Preparing the ricotta In a bowl, mix the ricotta with a little salt and water to create a smooth cream. Set aside.

Preparing the pizza base Begin with dough that has been allowed to rise properly. Roll out the dough ball on a lightly floured surface, forming a slightly raised edge around the sides (see page 15). Lift onto a baking sheet.

Adding the toppings Spread the ricotta mixture evenly over the pizza base, avoiding the edges.

Initial baking Place the pizza at the bottom of the preheated oven (see page 10) and bake for about 5 minutes. Do not allow the ricotta to dry out.

Adding the cheese After the initial 5 minutes of baking, when the base is nearly but not fully cooked, remove the pizza from the oven and add the pieces of fior di latte.

Final baking Transfer the pizza to the upper part of the oven and switch to the grill/broil mode. Cook for about 2 minutes, or until the cheese has melted and the crust is lightly golden.

Finishing and serving Remove the pizza from the oven, and finish with smoked salmon and a sprinkle of snipped chives. Add a drizzle of extra virgin olive oil. Let the pizza rest for a minute before slicing and serving.

1 ball Pizza Dough (see pages 12–15)
flour, for dusting
50 g/2 oz. ricotta
80 g/3 oz. fior di latte, torn into pieces
100 g/3½ oz. sliced smoked salmon/lox
a handful of fresh chives, snipped
extra virgin olive oil, to drizzle
salt

Dolci e bevande
DESSERTS & DRINKS

amarena cherry cheesecake

Delicious sour-sweet cherries in syrup top a creamy no-bake cheesecake, making an indulgent dessert to finish any meal.

Preparing the base Put the crushed digestive biscuits in a bowl and add the melted butter. Mix well until combined. Press the mixture firmly into the bottom of the springform tin to form a biscuit/cookie base. Chill in the refrigerator while you prepare the filling.

Making the filling In a large bowl, combine the mascarpone, cream, sugar and vanilla extract. Beat with an electric mixer until smooth and creamy.

Assembling the cheesecake Pour the filling over the chilled base and smooth the top with a spatula. Refrigerate for at least 4 hours, or until the cheesecake is set. Once set, release the cheesecake from the springform tin and slide it onto a serving plate.

Finishing and serving Before serving, top the cheesecake with whipped cream (if using) and spoon over the Amarena cherries and their syrup to glaze. Cut into slices and serve chilled.

BASE
250 g/9 oz. digestive biscuits/graham crackers, crushed
100 g/7 tablespoons unsalted butter, melted

FILLING
500 g/1 lb. 2 oz. mascarpone
200 ml/¾ cup double/heavy cream
100 g/½ cup granulated sugar
1 teaspoon vanilla extract

TOPPING
100 ml/⅓ cup double/heavy cream, whipped (optional)
Amarena cherries in syrup (approx 30)

a 22-cm/9-inch springform tin/pan (no need to grease or line)

SERVES 8–10

pistachio cheesecake

This luxurious treat features a rich pistachio cheesecake layer, topped with chopped nuts and drizzles of pistachio cream – a must for all pistachio lovers!

Preparing the base Put the crushed digestive biscuits in a bowl and add the melted butter. Mix well until combined. Press the mixture firmly into the bottom of the springform tin to form a biscuit/cookie base. Chill in the refrigerator while you prepare the filling.

Making the filling In a large bowl, combine the mascarpone, cream, sugar and vanilla extract. Beat with an electric mixer until smooth and creamy. Fold in the pistachio cream, mixing gently to ensure even distribution throughout the filling.

Assembling the cheesecake Pour the filling over the chilled base and smooth the top with a spatula. Refrigerate for at least 4 hours, or until the cheesecake is set. Once set, release the cheesecake from the springform tin and slide it onto a serving plate.

Finishing and serving Before serving, top the cheesecake with whipped cream (if using), drizzle over some pistachio cream and sprinkle with chopped pistachios. Cut into slices and serve chilled.

BASE
250 g/9 oz. digestive biscuits/graham crackers, crushed
100 g/7 tablespoons unsalted butter, melted

FILLING
500 g/1 lb. 2 oz. mascarpone
200 ml/¾ cup double/heavy cream
100 g/½ cup granulated sugar
1 teaspoon vanilla extract
200 g/7 oz. pistachio cream (available to buy in a jar), plus extra to finish

TOPPING
100 ml/⅓ cup double/heavy cream, whipped (optional)
50 g/½ cup chopped pistachios

a 22-cm/9-inch springform tin/pan (no need to grease or line)

SERVES 8–10

classic tiramisù

Perhaps the best known and most popular of all Italian desserts – here is my recipe.

Making the mascarpone filling In a large mixing bowl, whisk the egg yolks with the granulated sugar until light and fluffy. Add the mascarpone and Marsala (if using) and continue to whisk until the mixture is smooth and well combined. In a separate bowl, beat the egg whites until stiff peaks form. Gently fold the beaten whites into the mascarpone mixture until fully incorporated.

Assembling the tiramisù Quickly dip half the savoiardi sponge fingers into the cooled coffee, ensuring they are moistened but not soggy. Layer the dipped sponge fingers in a single layer at the bottom of a rectangular serving dish. Spread half the mascarpone mixture over the sponge fingers. Repeat with another layer of dipped fingers and top with the remaining mascarpone mixture. Smooth the top with a spatula.

Chilling Cover the dish with cling film/plastic wrap and refrigerate for at least 4 hours, or overnight to allow the flavours to meld and the tiramisù to set.

Finishing and serving Before serving, dust the top liberally with unsweetened cocoa powder and sprinkle with dark chocolate shavings if desired. Cut into squares and serve chilled.

400 ml/1¾ cups strong brewed black coffee, cooled
300 g/10½ oz. savoiardi sponge fingers/lady fingers
unsweetened cocoa powder, for dusting
dark/bittersweet chocolate shavings, to decorate (optional)

FILLING
4 UK large/US extra-large eggs, separated
100 g/½ cup granulated sugar
500 g/1 lb. 2 oz. mascarpone
30 ml/2 tablespoons Marsala wine (optional)

a medium rectangular dish or pan, approx. 23 x 35 cm/9 x 13 inches

SERVES 8–10

pistachio tiramisù

A sophisticated variation on the Classic Tiramisù (see page 159), with the addition of velvety pistachio cream.

Preparing the milk mixture In a bowl, mix the milk with the brandy or liqueur. Set aside.

Making the mascarpone mixture In a mixing bowl, beat the egg yolks with the granulated sugar until the mixture becomes pale and creamy. Add the mascarpone and pistachio cream to the egg yolk mixture. Mix until smooth and well combined.

Beating the egg whites Place the egg whites in a clean, dry bowl. Using clean beaters, whip the egg whites until they form stiff peaks.

Combining the mixtures Gently fold the beaten egg whites into the mascarpone-pistachio mixture until fully incorporated.

Assembling the tiramisù Quickly dip half the savoiardi sponge fingers into the milk and brandy mixture, ensuring they are moistened but not soggy. Arrange in the bottom of a serving dish. Spread half the mascarpone-pistachio mixture over the layer of sponge fingers. Repeat with another layer of dipped fingers and top with the remaining mascarpone mixture. Smooth the top with a spatula.

Chilling Cover the dish with cling film/plastic wrap and refrigerate for at least 4 hours, or overnight to allow the flavours to meld and the tiramisù to set.

Finishing and serving Just before serving, drizzle with extra pistachio cream and sprinkle over the chopped pistachios. Cut into squares and serve chilled.

200 ml/¾ cup milk
1 tablespoon brandy (or other liqueur of your choice)
3 UK large/US extra-large eggs, separated
250 g/9 oz. mascarpone
100 g/½ cup granulated sugar
100 g/3½ oz. pistachio cream (available to buy in a jar), plus extra to finish
200 g/7 oz. savoiardi sponge fingers/lady fingers
50 g/2 oz. shelled pistachios, finely chopped

a small rectangular dish or pan, approx. 20 x 31 cm/8 x 12 inches

SERVES 6

torta caprese

This traditional baked chocolate and almond cake is popular all over Italy, but especially in Naples.

Preheating the oven Preheat the oven to 180°C/350°F/Gas 4.

Melting the chocolate Break the dark chocolate into pieces and melt it gently using a double boiler or microwave. Once melted, set aside to cool slightly.

Preparing the nut mixture In a food processor, pulse the blanched almonds and walnuts until finely ground. Be careful not to over-process into a paste.

Mixing the batter In a large bowl, cream the softened butter with half the sugar until light and fluffy. Add the egg yolks one at a time, incorporating well after each addition. Stir in the melted chocolate, vanilla extract and the ground nuts. In a separate bowl, beat the egg whites with a pinch of salt until foamy. Gradually add the remaining sugar and continue beating until stiff peaks form. Gently fold the beaten egg whites into the chocolate mixture in three additions, being careful not to deflate the mixture.

Baking the cake Pour the batter into the prepared tin and smooth the top. Bake in the preheated oven for about 40–50 minutes, or until a cocktail stick/toothpick inserted into the centre comes out clean.

Finishing and serving Let the cake cool in the pan for 10 minutes, then remove the sides of the springform tin and allow it to cool completely on a wire rack. Dust with icing sugar before serving with whipped cream or vanilla ice cream and fresh berries, if liked.

150 g/5½ oz. dark/bittersweet chocolate (at least 70% cocoa)
150 g/1½ cups blanched almonds, finely ground
150 g/1½ cups walnuts, finely chopped
150 g/1¼ sticks unsalted butter, softened, plus extra for greasing
150 g/¾ cup granulated sugar
4 UK large/US extra-large eggs, separated
1 teaspoon vanilla extract
a pinch of salt
icing/confectioner's sugar, for dusting

TO SERVE (OPTIONAL)
whipped cream or vanilla ice cream
fresh berries

a 23-cm/9-inch springform tin/ pan, greased and base-lined with parchment paper

SERVES 8–10

mini sticky toffee puddings with hazelnut crumble & caramel cream

A much-loved English dessert, given a little Italian love...

Preheating the oven Preheat the oven to 180°C/350°F/Gas 4.

Making the batter In a bowl, combine the chopped dates and boiling water. Stir in the bicarbonate of soda and let sit for about 10 minutes. In a separate bowl, cream the butter and sugar until light and fluffy. Beat in the eggs one at a time, then mix in the vanilla extract. Fold the date mixture into the creamed butter. Sift in the flour and baking powder and mix until just combined.

Baking Divide the batter among the prepared muffin cups or ramekins, filling each about three-quarters full. Bake in the preheated oven for 20–25 minutes or until a skewer inserted into the centre comes out clean.

Making the hazelnut crumble Combine the hazelnuts, oats, brown sugar and melted butter in a bowl. Mix until well combined. Spread the mixture onto a baking sheet and bake in the oven at 180°C/350°F/Gas 4 for 10–15 minutes, stirring occasionally, until golden and crispy.

Preparing the caramel cream In a saucepan, melt the sugar over a medium heat until it turns a deep amber colour. Carefully stir in the butter (be cautious of splattering). Remove from the heat and slowly pour in the cream and vanilla extract, stirring continuously until smooth. Set aside to cool slightly.

Finishing and serving Once the puddings are baked and slightly cooled, remove them from the muffin pan or ramekins. Drizzle each pudding with warm caramel, top with a spoonful of hazelnut crumble and add a scoop of banana ice cream to serve.

180 g/6½ oz. dates, stoned/pitted and chopped
200 ml/¾ cup boiling water
1 teaspoon bicarbonate of soda/ baking soda
85 g/6 tablespoons unsalted butter, softened, plus extra for greasing
170 g/¾ cup plus 1½ tablespoons granulated sugar
2 UK large/US extra-large eggs
1 teaspoon vanilla extract
180 g/1⅓ cups plain/all-purpose flour
1 teaspoon baking powder
banana ice cream, to serve

HAZELNUT CRUMBLE
50 g/½ cup hazelnuts, chopped
50 g/½ cup porridge/rolled oats
50 g/¼ cup brown sugar
50 g/3½ tablespoons unsalted butter, melted

CARAMEL CREAM
100 g/½ cup granulated sugar
50 g/3½ tablespoons unsalted butter
120 ml/½ cup double/heavy cream
1 teaspoon vanilla extract

a muffin pan or 8–10 individual ramekins, greased

SERVES 8–10

sbriciolata alla Nutella

This crumbly and buttery cake, filled with the iconic chocolate hazelnut spread, is perfect with a cup of coffee.

Preheating the oven Preheat the oven to 180°C/350°F/Gas 4.

Making the crumble dough In a large mixing bowl, combine the flour, sugar, baking powder and a pinch of salt. Add the cold, cubed butter and use your fingers or a pastry cutter to blend the butter into the flour mixture until it resembles coarse crumbs. Stir in the egg and vanilla extract until the mixture is just combined but still crumbly. Do not overmix.

Assembling the cake Press about two-thirds of the crumble mixture into the bottom of the prepared tin to form a firm base. Spread the Nutella or chocolate-hazelnut spread evenly over the base, leaving a small margin around the edges to prevent sticking. Crumble the remaining dough over the chocolate-hazelnut layer.

Baking Place the pan in the preheated oven and bake for about 30–35 minutes, or until the top is golden and firm.

Finishing and serving Allow the cake to cool in the tin on a wire rack before removing. Once cool, dust with a little icing sugar. Cut into slices to serve.

300 g/2¼ cups plain/all-purpose flour
150 g/¾ cup granulated sugar
½ teaspoon baking powder
a pinch of salt
150 g/1¼ sticks cold unsalted butter, cubed
1 UK large/US extra-large egg
1 teaspoon vanilla extract
300 g/10½ oz. Nutella or other chocolate-hazelnut spread
icing/confectioner's sugar, to dust

a 23-cm/9-inch round baking tin/ pan, lined with parchment paper

SERVES 8–10

DRINKS

Italy is well-known for its delicious food and incredible wines, but it's also home to some classic cocktails. Whether you're a connoisseur or a newbie, we're sure you'll find something to enjoy in our small selection, from aperitivo hour spritzes to stronger tipples to sip after dinner.

aperol spritz

This classic is made with three parts Prosecco to two parts Aperol and one part soda water.

75 ml/2½ oz. Prosecco
50 ml/1⅔ oz. Aperol
25 ml/⅔ oz. soda water
ice cubes
an orange slice, to garnish

SERVES 1

Fill a large wine glass with ice cubes and pour the Prosecco over the ice. Pour the Aperol into the glass and add the soda water. Gently stir the mixture with a spoon to combine the ingredients. Garnish with a slice of orange and serve at once.

raspbellini

A raspberry twist on the classic peach Bellini, fresh and fruity!

30 ml/2 tablespoons raspberry purée
chilled Prosecco, to top up
15 ml/½ oz. raspberry Schnapps (optional)

SERVES 1

Pour the raspberry purée into a flute glass and top up with chilled Prosecco. If you wish to make the cocktail a little stronger, add the raspberry Schnapps. Serve at once.

amalfi spritz

This Italian cocktail is similar to an Aperol Spritz (see left) but with a refreshing lemony twist. It is made with three main ingredients, including homemade agave limonata.

50 ml/1⅔ oz. limoncello
50 ml/1⅔ oz. homemade agave limonata
**   (see below)**
Prosecco, to top up
a small fresh basil sprig and a lemon wedge,
**   to garnish**

SERVES 1

Pour the limoncello, limonata and Prosecco into a large wine glass filled with a few ice cubes. Give the ingredients a quick stir, then garnish with lemon slices and basil leaves to give aromatic notes. Serve at once.

Agave limonata In a large jug/pitcher, stir together 350 ml/1½ cups freshly squeezed lemon juice, 75 ml/3 fl oz. agave syrup and 1.5 litres/6 cups water. Add a whole sliced lemon to the mix and let it rest until you are ready to make cocktails, on enjoy as it comes!

basil gimlet

This delicious twist on the classic gimlet is the perfect refreshingly herbal drink for spring and summer.

50 ml/1⅔ oz. basil-infused gin
15 ml/½ oz. Amaretto Disaronno
20 ml/4 teaspoons freshly squeezed lime juice
5 ml/1 teaspoon sugar syrup
dried basil leaves (see below), to garnish

SERVES 1

Pour all the ingredients in a cocktail shaker and shake vigorously. Double strain into a coupette glass and garnish with dried basil leaves. Serve at once.

Dried basil leaves Place a handful of fresh basil leaves on a clean baking sheet and place in the oven. Turn the oven to its lowest temperature and leave for 30 minutes, then turn off the heat. Leave the oven door shut and let the leaves dry out for 10 hours or so.

the godfather

Named after the classic 70s movie, this drink is simply perfect to serve for both aperitivo and after dinner with its nutty notes and smoothness from the whisky.

50 ml/1⅔ oz. Scotch whisky
25 ml/⅔ oz. Amaretto Disaronno
an orange peel, to garnish

SERVES 1

Fill a mixing glass two-thirds full with cubed ice. Pour in the whisky and Amaretto Disaronno and stir until well chilled.

Strain into a rocks glass over fresh cubed ice. Garnish with an orange peel and serve at once.

garibaldino

The most authentic and easy-to-make cocktail Italy has to offer.

50 ml/1⅔ oz. Campari
5 ml/1 teaspoon sugar syrup
freshly squeezed orange juice, to top up
orange wedge, to garnish

SERVES 1

Place two ice cubes in a highball glass and add the Campari. Add a little of the orange juice to the glass and stir to combine. Add another ice cube and the remainder of the orange juice. Garnish with an orange wedge and serve at once.

porcini negroni

Mushrooms cocktails are now a thing! That's why we wanted to make a twist on the most classic Italian cocktail. Our porcini Negroni is incredibly easy to make, but its flavour punch is gobsmacking.

30 ml/1 oz. porcini mushroom-infused gin
   (see below)
20 ml/⅔ oz. red Vermouth
15 ml/½ oz. Campari
dried porcini mushroom, to garnish

SERVES 1

Pour all the ingredients into a rocks glass with ice cubes and stir well. Garnish the drink with a dried porcini mushroom and serve at once.

Porcini mushroom-infused gin Select a very basic gin with no added flavour. Add 100 g/3½ oz. dried porcini mushrooms to the bottle and let it rest for at least 48 hours before using.

index

acknowledgements

These are some people I'd really love to thank for everything they have done for me during my career, and for all the support they have shown me.

To Franco Anatriello, the person who has supported and believed in me more than anyone else in my life. I will love you forever.

To Lucrezia, who has been a driving force from day one. None of this would have been possible without you. You will always hold a special place in my life.

To my mother Francesca, my father Gerardo, and my entire family — thank you for supporting me and allowing me the freedom to make my own choices throughout my life. I love you all.

My heartfelt thanks to my business partners, Gianni and Massimo, for believing in me and supporting me every day.

A special thanks to Rosario Dello Iacovo for retelling my story in these pages — the book wouldn't be the same without your contribution.

Thank you to my publishers Ryland Peters & Small for making this book happen: Julia Charles Editorial Director, Leslie Harrington Creative Director, Megan Smith (for book design and art direction), Gillian Haslam (for copyediting) photographer Steven Joyce (for capturing such amazing images), Jess Geddes (for the beautiful food styling) and Hannah Wilkinson (for the great props).

Last but certainly not least, thanks to my incredible team at Napoli on the Road — I couldn't have accomplished any of this without you all. Special thanks go to Andrea Principessa for making the drinks for the photography.

picture credits